What Have You Done?

What Have You Done?

The Inside Stories of Auditioning—
from the Ridiculous to the Sublime

Edited by Louis Zorich

Limelight Editions
An Imprint of Hal Leonard Corporation
New York

Published in 2009 by Limelight Editions
An Imprint of Hal Leonard Corporation
7777 West Bluemound Road
Milwaukee, WI 53213

Trade Book Division Editorial Offices
19 West 21st Street, New York, NY 10010

Printed in the United States of America

Book design by Snow Creative Services

Library of Congress Cataloging-in-Publication Data

What have you done? : the inside stories of auditioning–
from the ridiculous to the sublime / edited by Louis Zorich.
    p. cm.
 Includes bibliographical references.
 ISBN 978-0-87910-365-1 (alk. paper)
 1. Actors–United States–Anecdotes. 2. Auditions–Anecdotes.
I. Zorich, Louis, 1924-
 PN2071.A92W43 2009
 792.0'280922–dc22
                                    2009032216

www.limelighteditions.com

To Olympia Dukakis, my wonderful wife, whose passion, love and piercing intelligence, never-ending curiosity and boundless loyalty, still amaze and surprise me after all these forty-three years

To my children, Christina, Peter, and Stefan, and their children, Isabella, Sofia, and Luka, for their love and affection

Contents

Two: What??

Three: Get the Job   57

Four: Nervous?   83

Seven: Making an Impression

Foreword

Once during the late sixties, Louie and I were racing down Eighth Avenue late for auditions. I was putting on earrings, complaining that my clothes were totally wrong, all the while urging Louie to move faster and faster. People were rushing by, loud traffic as usual, when suddenly Louie stopped, grabbed my arm, and started shouting, "Who are these people? Who do you think will be the room? Why are you behaving like this? Who are you? And who are they?"

The truth is that Louie has never stopped asking those questions, has never lost interest in the contradictions that give rise to those questions.

Dramatically opposed to the "interactive audition" is what I call the "spaceship"— tapings in quiet rooms with disembodied voices piped in. You almost expect the forks and cups to come floating by. There is no "they" in the room—the "they" are in their office in L.A. miles away, not burdened by your presence. The "they" is now an "IT," the camera.

My favorite story here is about my brother Apollo Dukakis who rented a studio, put himself on tape, sent it to the director of *Homebody/Kabul* and got the job! The opportunity to take matters into our hands, to take some control, is of course, an advantage.

The stories collected here are often outrageous, ridiculous, cruel, endearing, painful, but always, they exist as clues, symptoms, manifestations of who we are and who the "theys" are in the course of our lives as we seek to find and do the work to which we are so passionately drawn. How we come to see ourselves, how others see us and respond—how these disappoint or meet our expectations.

Once after a particularly disappointing audition, Louis asked me to describe what I did from the moment I entered the room. "Nothing," I said."I was introduced, found a chair, sat down in front of 'them' and began." He looked at me very carefully and said, "Olympia, you want only to prove that you're accomplished. But they want to know who you are. They know you're good, as are many others. What they don't know is anything about who you are and whether or not they want to spend four weeks with you." Who were the "theys" this time and what was I so defended against? This conversation has transpired between us many times over the last four-odd decades.

Louis has laughed uproariously about "who are they?" and "who are you?" questions. I've seen him stunned by recognition, deeply pained by revelations, but always his curiosity, his honesty, and his love of acting and actors has moved him forward.

We, all actors, have no job security—one show ends, the next must be found and more importantly, won. In *What Have You Done?*, Louie is showing something of who actors are, and the many "theys" we confront in our lives and in our work.

Olympia Dukakis

Preface

Why, you may ask, do they ask, "What have you done?" Because they, the producers and directors, haven't seen your work lately or maybe never. They don't know—so they ask you to show them what you can do . . . on a bare stage, a room or maybe in front of twenty people. You are about to audition.

Auditions can be and often are, well, let's say, odd experiences. Yes, many are well run, business-like, "Next!" affairs, and some are "give and take" where a director will actually have you try different approaches, and he'll work with you. This does not happen too frequently. Then some auditions you just connect with immediately, you know it, you can feel it. The part is yours. You own it. Then there are those auditions that are unnerving, anxiety-making. They happen more often than not, some actors feel it when first starting out, other actors always feel it, it doesn't seem to get better. You know the symptoms.

As you're about to read, you're aware that you have no feeling in your legs, in fact, you have no legs: "Where did they go?" Your hands holding the script are shaking, the Sahara Desert in your mouth is no help and you have to go to the toilet even though you just went before you came in.

But you pull yourself together, you get a grip. You keep auditioning, hundreds of times. You persist through the auditions you weren't right for, last-minute auditions that you "winged." The time you auditioned resentfully because of a two-hour wait, but you begin to get good at them. I truly believe that you never get a job because of that one audition, you get it because of *all* the auditions you ever had. You have to keep banging away. The only way is to get up there on your feet, face your demons, your insecurities, and fight through them. It gets easier. Fear is good.

And you know you're getting close when it's between you and a *name*, you have arrived at a tricky place. If it happens often enough, you or the name, you might think of getting a publicity person. Get *your* name out there. It's an expensive option.

There will come a time when it'll all come together, your talent, training, experience, being right for the part, and above all, knowing yourself, trusting yourself enough to dare, to not be afraid to challenge yourself, not be afraid to make mistakes. And when it happens they won't be asking you, "What have you done?" They will make you an offer without your auditioning because they'll know *what you have done.*

Acknowledgments

Special thanks to our personal assistant and all around friend Bonnie Low-Kramen, for her advice, guidance and just plain hard work that made this book possible. And to Robert Sanders who made everything so much easier. And to my mentor Elda Rotor Zorich, from Oxford University Press, for her publishing savvy, insights, and professional help. Thanks to Susan Day for her work on the early version of the book. Grateful thanks to the copy editor, Laura Sassano, and a heartfelt thanks to the omnipresent Jessica Burr for all her insight and knowledge in getting the book done. A special thank-you to Michael Messina, who first saw the possibilities of the book and, you might say, green-lighted it. And I must express my gratitude to my agent Bob Shuman, who introduced me to Messina and Limelight Editions, thus setting the wheels in motion.

Thanks to Bill Jones; without his initial enthusiasm, there would be no book. To my old friend James Cavanaugh, who helped point the way. My gratitude and love to Dr. Bella Itkin and Joe Slowik, teachers from the old Goodman Theatre School, for believing in me. To the late Walter Beakel, under whose direction I blossomed as an actor. Thanks to Nikos Psacharopoulos, artistic director for many years at the Williamstown Theatre Festival, whose love of Chekhov awakened me to all his plays. Thanks to Austin Pendleton, playwright, actor, director, teacher, and long-time friend, who does it all with panache.

What Have You Done?

"Thank you, Mr. Mulvaney, but what we're really looking for is
someone with talent."

Chapter One

You Won't Believe This

Meryl Streep

When Meryl was first auditioning for a part in a Dino De Laurentiis film, Dino turned to one of his associates and said in Italian, "What is she, what is she? She's not beautiful." Unknown to the room, Meryl spoke fluent Italian.

Calista Flockhart

Ally McBeal star Calista Flockhart will never forget the audition where she nearly fainted. The man she was auditioning for had taken his shoes off. "I thought it was his feet, they really smelled," she told Jay Leno. "It was terrible, I thought I was going to pass out. He kept me reading the scene over and over, and I was, like, going to die!"

In the subway on the way home, Calista crossed her legs and looked down at her shoe. It was covered with dog shit! "I was the one who was smelling up the room!"

Robert Mitchum

1. Hollywood is where everyone you meet is thinking, "So what can you do for me?" But the Hollywood producer is the ultimate extreme. You've probably heard the one about the starlet who offers the producer oral sex in return for a bit role, and he says to her, "But what's in it for me?"

2. The second movie Mitchum ever auditioned for was a Western. He had to ride a horse, which he had never done. The pony threw him, made him look bad, so Mitchum punched the horse, its eyes rolled back into his head . . . he got the part.

Richard Rodgers

The legendary music publisher Max Dreyfus granted Rodgers an audition at the request of Lawrence Schwab, a potential producer seeking a musical team for a play he was producing. Dreyfus, a formidable figure in the world of music publishing, discovered and promoted Jerome Kern and George Gershwin. At Rodgers's audition he dismissed Rodgers's music as having "nothing there."

Ironically, Dreyfus later became Rodgers and Hart's publisher.

Federico Fellini

Fellini, casting for the lead actor in his 1960 movie, *La Dolce Vita*, told Marcello Mastroianni that he needed a face with no personality in it "like yours." Instead of a script, Fellini sent him a rude cartoon, and Mastroianni accepted the part.

Kevin Spacey

At age fourteen, Kevin knew what he wanted to do with his life. The catalyst? Jack Lemmon's riveting performance in *Juno and the Paycock* at the Taper Forum in L.A. After the show, Kevin, overcome with awe, tremulously asked Jack for his autograph and guidance on how to become an actor. Jack paternally said to get training and to never give up.

Years later, in New York, Kevin did exactly that and when Jack came to do *A Long Day's Journey into Night*, Kevin got to audition for the older son and the unusual happened. Kevin, reading with his favorite actor, idol, and teacher took Jack on. He slugged it out with him, blow by blow, line by line, scene by scene, and when the bell rang, Kevin had the part.

Klaus Kinski

Klaus, desperate for work, and hungry, tries to see Wolfgang Langhoff, the artistic director of Max Reinhardt's Deutsches Theatre in East Berlin. Weeks passed. Months. Nothing. Finally he was called in to audition. Klaus threw himself into the reading, screaming, weeping his eyes out, banging his hands and arms till they were bloody. Langhoff didn't even listen as he wolfed down sandwiches and rubbed a spot of sugary tea from his tie.

"Come back in a few years," he said, "maybe something will work out. And eat. Eat, eat! You're so skinny, people are worried you're going to be shattered by your own emotional eruptions. So eat!"

Michael Gambon

Michael Gambon and Brian Cox shared a dressing room for a full season at Birmingham. The last show of the year was *Othello*, Michael playing the title role, Brian playing Iago. Frequently, Brian would tell Michael about a new series he was soon to do for the BBC, called *The Borderers*.

One evening, Brian told Michael the series's producers were coming to see the show. After the show, they came backstage and Brian ducked behind the door when they knocked. Michael opened it. They identified themselves. Michael said, "Brian is here."

Whereupon they asked Michael to step out into the corridor . . . and offered him, Michael, the part.

Michael went back into the dressing room, and to a depressed Brian, saying, "I'm sorry, mate."

Marlon Brando

1. After a year of *I Remember Mama* on the New York stage, Marlon wanted to move on to other roles. His agent set up an audition for *O Mistress Mine*, an Alfred Lunt–Lynn Fontanne comedy. As usual, Marlon slouched onstage, unshaven, unkempt, and uncooperative. Lunt gave him the script, saying, "Pick out a few lines and read them." Marlon squinted for several moments, then threw the script into the fifth row. "I can't do it," he said.

"Try something from memory," said the patient, ever-helpful Mr. Lunt.

Marlon thought, struggled and strained. Finally he spoke up. "Hickory, Dickory Dock, the mouse ran up the clock."

2. In Tahiti's Grand Hotel, Marlon was auditioning women for the part of the native girlfriend of Mr. Christian for the movie *Mutiny on the Bounty*. Auditioning in his hotel room, as each one entered, Marlon was out on the window ledge of the top story shouting, "I've had it, I'm jumping out the window."

Every woman who came in couldn't stop giggling at Marlon's suicide attempt. An eighteen-year-old waitress from the hotel was chosen for the part . . . she giggled the least.

Gary Merrill

Gary, during his early radio days, tells of an actor friend who was short and ordinary looking, but had a beautiful, seductive voice. He was very well known and worked a lot. Asked for the secret of his success at auditions, he said: "I think 'cock' with every line."

Oliver Stone

Actor Julius Tennon is auditioning in a radio studio with Mr. Stone who is looking for voices for his film *Talk Radio* with

Eric Bogosian. Julius stands before a mike and Mr. Stone sits facing him behind a table on which is photos of the actors auditioning.

Mr. Stone holds Julius's picture before him and repeats his name—Julius Tennon, Julius Tennon, Julius Tennon, and Julius Tennon . . . oh, about ten or fifteen times as Julius stands poised ready to record. Finally, Mr. Stone's assistant gives Julius a nod and he proceeds to read. A minute or two into the reading, Mr. Stone slides off his chair and slips under the table, disappearing completely.

Julius waits for a response. There is none. He waits—still no Mr. Stone. His assistant gives some sort of sign to Julius who leaves the room with Mr. Stone somewhere under the table.

Tennessee Williams / Marlon Brando

When Edith Van Cleve was sent a copy of Tennessee Williams's *A Streetcar Named Desire,* she instantly felt it was ideally suited for her client Marlon Brando. Marlon agreed. The producer, Irene Selznick, did not agree, nor did the director Elia Kazan. Mrs. Selznick announced she had signed John Garfield. Garfield, however, after some thought felt that the role of Stanley Kowalski was overshadowed by that of Blanche DuBois, and he bowed out. Burt Lancaster was the next name to come up—but he had a conflict.

With time running out and Miss Van Cleve's persistence, Kazan and Selznick agreed to audition Marlon. But Miss Van Cleve said no. She sensed Marlon might come shuffling in with a kimono, false buckteeth and a Japanese accent, or some such crazy caper. It was then agreed that Marlon would be signed without an audition *if* the playwright approved.

At the time, Tennessee was holed up in a cottage on the beach in Provincetown, Massachusetts fine-tuning the play. Williams recalls the incident:

"I had very little money at the time, and was living in this broken-down house. I had a houseful of people; the plumbing was flooded and someone had blown the light fuse. Someone said a kid named Brando was down on the beach and looked good. He arrived in the evening, wearing Levis, took one look at the confusion around him and went to work. First he stuck his hand into the overflowing toilet bowl and unclogged the drain, then he tackled the fuses. Within an hour, everything worked. Then he read the script aloud, just as he played it. It was the most magnificent reading I ever heard. And he had the part immediately. He stayed the night, slept curled up with an old quilt in the center of the floor."

Peter Riegert

One of Peter's first auditions is probably the most charming and ingenuous stories I've heard. He read for a play and afterward his agent asked him how it went. Peter told him he thought he got the job.

"How do you know?" asked his agent.

"They said, thank you very much."

Renée Zellweger

Presumably after auditioning for the part of Dorothy Boyd for the movie *Jerry Maguire*, starring Tom Cruise, Renée got a call from the picture's director, Cameron Crowe, notifying her that the part was hers. Renée said, "What makes you think I want it?"

Later she said she thought Cameron was kidding . . . he wasn't.

Theodor Komisarjevsky

Komisarjevsky, one-time Russian director of the imperial and state theatres, in 1947 came to New York with John Gielgud to direct him in *Crime and Punishment*. Hundreds of people lined up standing outside the theatre to audition on a terribly cold blizzard of a day.

Many of them were foreigners because, being a Russian play, accents did not matter, but strange to say, whenever a German or Jew came on to read, Komisarjevsky turned his back.

Susan Sarandon

In New York City about a week, Susan auditioned for a small-budget film. According to Susan, it was her first ever—and they hired her. "I never studied acting and I still haven't. So it goes to show you how difficult acting really is."

William Youmans

Bill is in Dallas in a show that opens the next night. He gets a call to fly to New York City to audition before Michael Crawford, star of the new Broadway musical *Dance of the Vampires*. Luckily, it's his day off. He flies to St. Louis, then boards another plane bound for New York City. As the planes leaves the gate and heads out on the tarmac, Bill is sitting in the back of the almost empty plane going over and over the songs. It's something about blood transfusions for the vampire and the scene builds to a climax.

Bill is now beginning to act out the scene, singing and gesturing alone in the back of the plane when suddenly he hears, "Excuse me, sir, are you okay? We're a little concerned. We saw you gesturing and kind of talking to yourself. Is everything okay?"

"No, no, I'm fine. I'm going over a part, I'm auditioning in New York and I'm kind of nervous. It's a chance to get a Broadway show . . . my first."

"Okay, no problem." The flight attendant leaves. The plane is rolling along the tarmac when the captain comes back, and sits next to Bill.

The captain: "Sir, are you all right? We're told you're acting strangely. Everything ok?"

Bill: "Oh, yes. I'm auditioning for this musical, see here's my script."

The captain: "Okay. Fine." He leaves.

Bill continues going over the music. Over the speaker comes an announcement: "Ladies and gentlemen, we're experiencing a slight technical problem—the red light on the panel is on—we're heading back to the gate—but very briefly, we should be on our way in no time." The plane turns around and heads for the gate.

Bill (jokingly to the flight attendant): "I hope it isn't me."

Attendant: "Oh, no, it's the red light, something's wrong on the plane."

They get to the gate. The door opens and two security men come on board and they sit next to Bill.

Security: "Sir, we hear you've been acting strangely. We're going to have to take you off the plane."

Bill shows them the script. He even acts out the scene he was working on, British accent and all.

"Sorry, but we really have to take you off the plane."

Bill can't understand why all this is happening when it occurs to him that it is post-9/11. But it still mystifies him. His only thought is the audition. He pulls out his cell phone, saying, "Here, I'll call my agent you can talk to him, you'll see."

Security: "No, we're not talking to your agent. Come along sir, you're making it much harder on yourself."

Bill is now off the plane. The plane leaves. They begin to lecture him on how he has ruined everyone's day, how thoughtless he was, making the passengers uncomfortable.

About this time they proceed to check Bill out, something they should have done on the plane. When Bill asked why, they said the captain did not want him on his plane. Apparently they were satisfied with Bill's story and he was cleared. They said they would arrange a later flight for Bill, but he would never have made it back in time for the opening in Dallas.

Bill missed the audition and his chance to make his debut on Broadway in *Dance of the Vampires*, which opened to bad reviews and closed shortly. However, had he gotten it he would've missed out on the hit show he made his debut in, *La Bohème*.

Bijou Phillips

"Late one night," recalls director J. Toback, "Leonardo DiCaprio called me up from the Bowery Bar and said, 'You've got to come right now and see this girl. Her name's Bijou, she's John Phillips's daughter, and she's crazy . . . phenomenal.' So I went. Leo and his male friends were there—Bijou was the only girl in the group – and she was dancing on top of a table. She was fourteen, but looked about eight. I made a mental note: When she's eighteen, I've got to use her."

Four years later, Toback did precisely that, casting Bijou, who had no previous film acting experience, as the lead "white kid" in *Black and White*, a heavily improvised movie.

"The audition was weird," remembers Bijou. "I showed up, and he was like, 'Hi, Bijou,' and we went to get some pizza. He had met me out one night and was enamoured. I was dancing with some hot chick. It was during my show-off period, and he, like, fell in love with me. I thought he was crazy, a pathological liar—just trying to get into my pants. I never thought he was going to give me the part."

Gower Champion

Gower disliked auditions. He found them unnatural and tough on actors. He felt some very fine actors could not for the life of them audition well. In a normal theatrical situation these actors were okay, but auditions were strange to go through and sometimes even bizarre for a director to watch.

Gower was seeing actors for the part of Jocko for the musical *Carnival*, when out came Pierre Olaf. Script in hand, peering at it with his tiny glasses. Suddenly his script came apart, falling like leaves everywhere over the stage floor. Somehow Pierre kept reading and continued by getting down on the floor, reading from the pages strewn all over . . . one page here, one page there.

Gower was amazed how this disaster of an audition turned out so well. Pierre was the perfect Jocko.

Paul Mazursky

Paul, directing the movie *Down and Out*, was auditioning dogs for a large part in the film. Into his office came Mike, a black and white Australian sheepdog and his trainer, Clint Rowe. Paul asked the dog to sit on the couch. Clint said something and Mike jumped up on the couch and sat facing Paul looking as if he knew he'd get the part. He wasn't the least bit nervous.

Clint began to ask Paul questions usually asked by actors. "How old do you see Mike in your show?" "Does he like Dave more than Barbara?" "Does he believe Jerry's stories?"

Sometimes Clint would say to Paul, "I don't think Mike would do that."

Paul was astounded. "You're telling me the dog wouldn't put his chin on Nick Nolte's leg? Why? Why not?"

Clint looked at Paul as if he were naïve and said, "Because he'd know Nick is lying in this situation."

"You're telling me a dog knows when someone is lying?" Paul asked.

Clint frowned. "Absolutely."

"My God, I'm working with a method dog!"

Mike almost stole the picture.

Michael Caine

Stanley Baker, the biggest tough-guy actor in British movies circa 1963, came to see Michael in a play in London where Michael played a comic Cockney. Baker was making his debut as a producer of a film about the Zulu wars at the end of the nineteenth century, and Michael was very right for a part of a Cockney soldier.

Michael first had to meet with Cy Endfield, an American director who knew little about the Zulu wars and even less about Cockneys. Endfield saw Michael and said, "Sorry . . . I don't think you're very good as a Cockney . . . my idea of a Cockney is a little, down-trodden, working-class man."

Of course, Michael was a Cockney and came from a poor, working-class background, but to Endfield, Michael looked too "aristocratic." Michael started to leave, felt very dejected, but was called back by Endfield, who felt it would be okay for Michael to play an officer who was Cockney . . . proving to Michael that Endfield knew nothing about class conflict in England.

It was Michael's first big break in the movies.

Andre Gregory

Gregory auditioned for and landed the role of John the Baptist in Scorsese's *The Last Temptation of Christ*. "Scorsese didn't know my work, and oddly he'd never seen *My Dinner with Andre*. He said to me, 'Do you know anything about shamans?' and I said, 'You're looking at one, Mr. Scorsese.' He smiled and said, 'Can you show me anything shaman-like?' and I said, 'If you can give me forty-five minutes to get into a trance state, sure.'

"So they came back forty-five minutes later, and I was completely naked, chanting and dancing. I was in a trance, so I didn't see that he went out of the room to get a movie camera.

"Afterwards, he said, 'I'm sending this to Hollywood, they've never seen an audition like this one.'"

Alec Guinness

In 1934 Guinness's audition for a small part in a production of Shakespeare's *Antony and Cleopatra* was greeted with a cry from the director: "You're no actor! Get off the fucking stage!"

Celeste Holm

They were casting the play *Habeas Corpus* in New York, and Celeste, very well known in theatre and film circles, was called in to read. She felt humiliated and angry to have to audition at this point in her career and she told the stage manager exactly how she felt.

"But everybody is auditioning," he said.

"This is a disgrace," she said.

"I'm sorry it's so," said the stage manager.

"Sorry won't do," she said.

"What if we sneak you in? We'll make sure no one will see."

At that moment Celeste sees someone on stage talking with the director, Frank Dunlop. Surprised, Celeste realizes it's Katharine Hepburn herself, who then exits the far side of the stage as Mr. Dunlop says, "Thank you for coming in Miss Hepburn."

Seeing this, Celeste acquiesces, beaming—even Katharine Hepburn had to audition. Little did she know that Hepburn was there checking out the theatre for her next show, *Coco*.

Robert Kalfin

Kalfin tells this story:

A young lady, dressed very colorfully in wildly colored tights with lots of scarves and bandanas hanging from her outfit, came in for a musical audition. She walked upstage, bent over with her rear end to us and placed various shopping bags and other objects on the floor there. Then she came downstage and placed a small tape recorder on the floor, pushed a button to start the music, then took center stage.

She began singing with the tape and as the musical number built to a chorus refrain, she proceeded to rotate continuously in a circle as she sang. We gently stopped her. Deeply upset, she cried out, "I paid a choreographer fifty dollars to prepare this audition, I've got to do the whole thing!" We signaled her to continue, for we felt for her.

She did, this time she began to rotate *counterclockwise* as she sang. Again we gently thanked her for coming in, but she gestured that there was *more*. She ran upstage, reached into her shopping bag, then came downstage again whirling in circles, as she sang with a bubble-pipe wand in one hand and a bottle of bubble mixture in the other, painting great arcs of bubbles in the air as she whirled and sang, turning first clockwise, then counterclockwise on alternate phrases of the refrain. We laughed good-naturedly. She signaled that there was more to come.

Finally the music started approaching the big finish. Once more she ran upstage, bent over her objects for a moment, then turned around to face us with two huge inflated balloons attached to her breasts.

She ran downstage towards us, still singing, then built to her big finish whirling clockwise on a phrase and breaking one balloon with a big slap of her hand to her chest, then whirling the other way and breaking the second balloon, followed by a big finale gesture and a bow.

We laughed a lot, thanked her for all the trouble she went to, told her it was memorable and that we'd be in touch.

Joe Sicardi

Very early in his acting career in New York, Joe had no luck getting an audition or work until one day he met a fellow actor leaving an audition. They talked—Joe was right for one of the parts. Sensing an opportunity, Joe decided to take a shot at it. He entered the building, saw actors waiting, preparing. He walked up to the assistant at the desk who asked his name.

Joe: "Joe Sicardi."

Assistant: (checking sheet): "Sorry, no Joe Sicardi."

Joe: "But my agent, William Morris, made the appointment and the time."

Assistant: "What can I tell you? You're not on the schedule."

Joe: "You have to be joking!"

Assistant: "Here's the sheet . . . where do you see Joe Sicardi?"

Joe: "Oh my God! I can't believe this! Someone screwed up!"

Assistant: "Where's your picture and resume?"

Joe: "What? They forgot to send them? What am I going to do?"(yelling) "I missed my doctor's appoinment to come here!!!"

Stage manager (entering): "What the hell is going on here?"

The assistant explains, the stage manager checks schedule: "Squeeze him in."

Not bad for an actor who had no appointment, no picture and resume, and William Morris was not his agent . . . in fact, he had no agent at all.

Judi Dench

At the end of the third year of London's Central School for Speech and Drama, students audition for the Outside World, London's theatrical agents and casting people. Among them was a rep from the Old Vic, that venerable institution, who was so impressed with Judi that she arranged an audition with its artistic head, Michael Benthall.

Judi read one of Miranda's speeches from the *Tempest*, and then was asked by Mr. Benthall to "go away and learn" Ophelia's speech from *Hamlet*, "O, what a noble mind is here o'erthrown?"

A few days later she returned and read. She was asked to go to Mr. Benthall's office to talk. Puzzled, she thought she was only there to get a job as a walk-on, but he talked about her height and . . . cast her as Ophelia—a part that forty other actresses were desperate to play opposite John Neville's Hamlet.

Treat Williams

While Treat was appearing in the Broadway musical *Grease*, word got around that Milos Forman was seeing people for the movie of *Hair*. Treat, very interested, called his agent about it. His agent said Forman was only seeing *Jesus Christ Superstar* people and rock and roll singers. Treat said, "I'm singing rock and roll in *Grease*."

The agent said, "That's fifties stuff!"

Treat said okay; then one night, an actor/singer from *Grease* told Treat he was auditioning for *Hair*. A week later two others from the show got auditions. Treat called and told his agent what was happening and if he didn't get an audition for *Hair* he'd fire him. He got the audition. Subsequently, Milos saw Treat in *Grease*, and upon meeting him Milos told Treat, "You do something very few actors do . . . you go completely overboard."

Now, the whole process begins. Milos would bring in different people in groups to read and Treat would audition each time with different actors. Then he'd go audition for the choreographer, Twyla Tharp, who ran him ragged. Treat would do the dance, then she'd say, "Can you do it again?" Treat felt it was more of a test of wills than an audition and that she wasn't testing his dance skills but his work ethic.

Jerry Ragni, one of the originators of the *Hair* book, and who played the lead on Broadway (the same part Treat was auditioning for in the movie), was around a lot during the auditions, hiding behind seats, watching. Treat began to hang around with him.

Treat then had to get the approval of the singing department, then the acting department, directing, dancing. He went back to Twyla three times, back to the music department four times. Over a period of a month, Treat was getting more and more frustrated. He kept asking himself, "Do I have it or not?"

Meanwhile they were doing a revival of *Hair* and they had final auditions for it, so Treat found himself auditioning both for the stage musical *and* the movie of *Hair*. There is an opening number where the lead character takes off his pants and is revealed in his jock strap. At this audition Treat was angry and tired when he learned that Jerry Ragni, who had originated and played the same part and played it all over the world, had reservations about Treat playing the part. He was sending mixed signals.

Treat began to sense that it was, to Ragni, his signature role, his fifteen minutes of fame, and although he was too old for the part now, he did not want to give it up.

With this on his mind, at the final audition, Treat launched into the opening speech, enraged. He took off his pants—no jock strap, stark naked, and very angry—and said, "Fuck you!" and mooned them.

Ragni came up to the stage saying, "What are you doing, man?" when Treat grabbed him yelling, "You have been fucking with my head, and I've had it, I don't want it anymore!" Treat wrestled Ragni to the floor of the stage, screaming at him, and the frustration of all the many auditions, the callbacks, the putting him through the wringer, came out.

Later, to Milos Forman, Treat tearfully said, "That's it, twelve auditions, I can't take it anymore."

Milos said, "You got the job."

Treat thought he had blown it, then realized his abandoning it, not wanting or needing it, got it for him . . . that and wrestling the part from Ragni, physically, emotionally, and psychically.

Betty Garrett

Betty, in the early forties in New York, worked as a singer/ dancer at places like the Latin Quarter and the World's Fair when luckily she auditioned for a revue called *All in Fun*, and got it. Betty, naturally, was terribly excited and nervous about her first featured part on Broadway. The role: Helen of Troy, with a terrific number to sing.

For four days she rehearsed her song over and over, but as she moved about the space she began to feel very odd . . . strange. She heard someone else singing her number in another room.

On the fifth day, the producer, Leonard Sillman, called four singers out on the stage and had each sing the same song, one after the other . . . then he fired three of them . . . including Betty.

Betty was shocked and humiliated. She begged to be allowed to stay, asking, "Why?" It was only later she found out that producers had the right to the five-day rule (i.e., they could keep or fire anyone in a five-day rehearsal period).

Betty had a measure of revenge. *All in Fun* was a big flop.

Lerner & Loewe

Alan Lerner and Fritz Loewe began working on the musical version of the George Bernard Shaw play *Pygmalion*, which later became *My Fair Lady*, on the condition that they could get Mary Martin for the part of Eliza. It was a star vehicle and the economics of Broadway demanded star casting.

Oddly enough, Oscar Hammerstein told Lerner, "It can't be done. Dick [Rodgers] and I worked on it for over a year and gave it up."

Nevertheless, Mary Martin and her manager-husband, Richard Halliday, agreed in November 1954 to listen to five songs Lerner and Loewe were ready to audition: Eliza's cheerfully spiteful "Just You Wait ('enry 'iggins)"; another Eliza song to precede the Embassy Ball, called "Say a Prayer for Me Tonight" (later dropped); plus two songs for Higgins; and, finally, "The Ascot Gavotte."

Martin's husband reported her reaction as "Those dear boys have lost their talent."

Loewe deadpanned, "I guess they didn't like it."

Hal Prince

Robert Kalfin was assisting Hal when they were casting the musical *Candide*. A young man came out on stage and started to sing. They listened for a while, then Hal stopped him and said, "You're really terrific, you're not right for this show, but I'm doing another musical later on that I think you're absolutely right for. You'll get the information and we'll call you in."

"And who are *you*?" asked the young man, grinning smartly.

"Prince," replied Mr. Prince.

"Prince *who*?" asked the young man, flashing his teeth.

"Never mind," said Mr. Prince.

Ginger Rogers

Ginger Rogers was in a wheelchair for about ten years and grew fat, according to Irving Fein, a celebrity manager. Then she started walking on her own and lost some weight. She was ready and willing to go back to work in mother and grandmother roles. Until she was interviewed by a young agent at CAA who asked her what pictures she had done. Ginger walked out of the meeting.

Gerry Jedd

This from Charles Nelson Reilly:

In the sixties, knocking around New York, was the late Ms. Jedd, a wonderfully vibrant actress. A friend who sold orange drinks at the then Alvin Theatre told her that they were reading for the part of Gittel in *Two for the Seesaw* in London with Peter Finch. He said, "I know the stage manager and you can get an appointment." Ms. Jedd read for Gittel and got the part. She then went to her agent and said, "They're reading for Gittel and . . ."—the agent interrupted with "Yes, and you are not right for it, that's why I didn't send you up for it."

David Black

David, at one time a performer himself and then later a Broadway producer of some eighteen shows, also taught and lectured on auditioning. Out of it, he wrote a very popular book, *The Actor's Audition*. Among some of his experiences: "I found myself staring in open-mouthed disbelief at the antics of actors auditioning.

"For one musical, an actress spent several minutes putting flowers all over the stage before beginning her song. Another showed up with her own brass band and her mother."

Jack Davidson

Jack was sent up for a national commercial to play a business-man. At the audition, the casting lady said, "What's with the beard?"

Jack explained: it was for a show that just closed out-of-town. He read for the part and left.

The next day his agent called, "Jack, you have a beard?"

"Yes, why?"

"The commercial casting lady called complaining about you auditioning for a businessman with a beard. Businessmen don't wear beards. Please get rid of it. It's embarrassing for all of us."

Jack shaved off the beard.

Later, he gets a call-back for the same commercial and its producer asks, "Where's the beard? We love it. We want the beard. You looked more interesting with it than the other actors."

"Well, the casting lady complained to my agent. I shaved it."

"Oh, well, that's too bad, because we wanted that beard, but thanks anyway for coming in."

Malachy McCourt

McCourt tells this story:

I was out in Hollywood auditioning for a TV show. The role: a priest—a prison chaplain—late 50s, gray-haired, heavy-set, ruddy complexion, blue-eyed Irish; Father O'Hara. I was going over the sides waiting to be called, when a female, who might have been verging on her fourteenth year, entered and told me to follow her. We went down a corridor and into a room.

I was gawking around furtively to see if there was a responsible adult present, when the diminutive one said she was Mindy and that I would be reading with her. As good an actor as I am, it was hard to conceal my astonishment that this mere child was going to judge my professional capabilities. We began the reading, when I was startled by a series of yelps from Mindy, to wit: What . . . what . . .what is this?

"What is what?" sez I, thinking that a rat had entered the room, she was so exercised.

"What is this dialect you're using?"

"That is not a dialect," sez I, "that is an accent."

"What's the difference?" bleated Mindy.

"An accent denotes a national origin, a dialect, a specific region of that nationality."

"Well, whatever it is, it won't do."

"The script says O'Hara is Irish," sez I.

"Not your kind of Irish," sez she.

I left rapidly lest I commit casticide.

James T. Cavanaugh

Cavanaugh shares this story:

I stage-managed the Broadway auditions for Norman Krasna's *We Interrupt This Program*. About half the roles were members of a black gang, which, forming the structure of the play, took over the John Golden Theatre, disrupting the performance of a silly comedy and holding the audience for ransom. The script called for some of the gang to patrol through the audience during much of the evening, automatic weapons in their hands, stockings over their faces.

The director, Jose Ferrer, grew to be concerned that the audience might be actually frightened, surrounded by gun-toting black men, so during the auditions he favored lighter-skinned actors, "café-au-lait," he called them, believing the audience would be less afraid of brown men than black men.

The producers, Alex Cohen and Hildy Parks, argued that the *best* actors should be chosen, regardless of their shade.

Their disagreement about the degrees of color intensified day by day. When they communicated it was never face to face. Their non-confrontational confrontation peaked when Ferrer grabbed his coat and without looking at Cohen, yelled, "You want a yes-man, Alex, not a director!"

As Ferrer was departing, Cohen leapt up and bellowed, "Joe, directors are a dime a dozen!"

The audition process was far more exciting than the play. It opened and closed very quickly.

William Devane

NBC thought they had a winner in their upcoming TV show *Cheers*. The lead part, Sam Malone, was yet to be cast. Devane was clearly the frontrunner with all his background and experience. It was set up for him to be tested on the *Cheers* set.

Devane, inexplicably, chose to wear casual pants and a t-shirt and to walk around bare-footed. During a scene in back of the bar, a glass fell and shattered on the floor, but Devane kept on playing the scene as if it didn't happen. But something did happen. He was thrown, his rhythm was off and it was clear to the producers that Devane was not the Devane they knew. He was spared the cuts to his feet; however, he had blown the audition.

The producers felt Devane did not want to come off as a "wimp," when the right thing to do would have been to stop the scene, clean up the broken glass and begin the scene again.

Devane lost the part to Ted Danson.

George London

Dramatic baritone George London toured with the Bel Canto Trio—London, soprano Frances Yeend, and tenor Mario Lanza—coast to coast. Back in New York, London worked on operatic roles. Realizing that the American opera scene afforded him opportunity for neither the artisitic growth he wanted nor the career leap he needed, London decided in 1949 to go to Europe.

Through colleagues, he was able to get a midnight post-performance audition with conductor Karl Böhm and the Wiener Staatsoper director, Franz Salmhofer, who, assuming Amonasro (*Aida*) to be in London's repertory, offered it to him as a debut role.

London, afraid to admit he didn't know the part, allowed the assumption to stand. He went out, worked on the part, and without any stage rehearsal made a triumphant debut.

Rocco Sisto

Sometime after leaving the NYU drama school, Rocco had an audition for Scorsese's *Raging Bull*, about the life of Jake LaMotta, an Italian-American boxer, starring Robert De Niro and Joe Pesci. Though it was a small part, on his third callback, Cis Corman, the casting director, said he was wrong for the part.

Rocco: "Why?"

Cis: "I'm looking for someone Italian."

Rocco: "But I was born in Bari, Italy."

Cis: "But we need someone who speaks Italian."

Rocco: "I speak fluent Italian."

Cis: "But we need someone who is more street."

Rocco: "I grew up on the New York streets."

(Pause . . . while looking at Rocco's picture and resume reading Shakespeare and his Chekhov's credits. . . .)

Cis: "I'm sorry, but you've done too many classics."

Josh Logan

Tony Randall at one time frequented a gym to work out and
would see Josh there. Josh, in the forties and fifties, was a
very successful New York director of plays (*Mr. Roberts*) and
musicals (*World of Suzie Wong, South Pacific*). Josh did not
work out, but he took steambaths. He told Tony he was in
the steamroom once, completely naked sitting next to a very
fat man with an extremely hairy body.

Putting his face right next to Logan's, the man said,
"You're Josh Logan, aren't you?" Josh nodded his head.

The man stood right up and burst into "One Alone" from
Sigmund Romberg's *Desert Song.*

Joseph Sommer

Waiting to be seen for a commercial, Joe became aware of
moans coming from the audition room, followed by sobs,
then loud screams, and more sobs. After a few minutes, the
door opened and the casting lady appeared with a dishev-
eled actor. She thanked him profusely and he left, mumbling
vague obscenities.

The casting lady ushered in another actor and what
followed were more screams, sobs, and moans. The door
opened and that actor left looking unhappy.

By now, for Joe, the audition room had become a chamber of horrors. He was next into the room, with no furni-
ture, only a video camera and monitor. On the floor were
a blanket and a pair of women's high-heeled shoes. The
casting lady explained that the commercial was concerned
with traffic safety. There was no script, only a situation from
which the actor was expected to improvise.

"I've asked to see only actors with strong acting credits,"
she said, "So the situation is . . . you've been to a cocktail
party and on the way home you've been responsible for

an accident in which your wife—that blanket roll and the shoes—has been killed.

"You don't realize, however, that she's dead. You kneel by her side and are surrounded by onlookers and police cars. With whirling red lights. A policeman is trying to move you away . . . your car radio is playing 'Melancholy Baby.' I'll run a tape of that to help you set the mood."

Joe's first impulse was to break out of the room. He stifled that. Next he thought to explain that his acting credits were really not that strong, nor was his stomach . . . but he felt he should give it a shot.

"You have almost sixty seconds for this in the actual spot, but take more time now if you need it."

Joe lost his last chance to escape by slating his name. He knelt next to the rolled up blanket. The casting lady, while working the camera, took on the role of the onlookers throwing out lines about how he caused the accident and the tape is playing, "Come to me, my melancholy baby, cuddle up and don't be blue."

It began to get to him. He carefully removed his wife's shoes to make her more comfortable. The casting lady was now the policeman trying to get him away as Joe shouted he would not leave his wife's side ever, ever.

"Every cloud must have a silver lining."

Whereupon Joe shed copious tears and stood up and said to the camera, "I cannot take anymore of this bizarre scene!" The casting lady turns off the camera and dissolved into a flood of tears.

"That was great, Joe," she sobbed, "really beautiful. I've seen fifteen today and they all have been so moving. I don't know how I'll get through tomorrow's sessions . . . don't go yet, wait until I'm sure the tape machine didn't mess up."

As the machine played and Joe saw himself speak his name, then on his knees before the red high heels, he ran out of the room so as not to see anymore of the act that he had just committed.

Jack Klugman

Auditioning for the part of Herbie in the original musical *Gypsy*, starring Ethel Merman on Broadway, Jack apparently so impressed the producers and director that they offered him the part on the spot.

Reportedly, Jack said, "I don't know if I can do it." When he was asked why not, Jack said, "I have to talk to my therapist first."

Barry Moss

Barry, of Hughes/Moss Casting in New York, relates:

We were doing a show called *Sherlock's Last Case* and a lady read for it. In the audience was the star and the director and they said, "She's fabulous, she's wonderful," and then she finished the scene and they said thank you, and she took the script and tore it to bits and said, "*Shit!*" and stormed offstage and lost the part. She just didn't like the way the reading went. But ironically they were going to offer her the part.

So I always advise people that you are auditioning from the moment you walk into the room until the moment you leave the room.

Timothy Carey

Timothy, an intense character actor in Hollywood (*Paths of Glory* with Kirk Douglas), was auditioning for Harry Cohn, head of Columbia Pictures, in the fifties. In the middle of the audition, he broke down and said, "This is so humiliating, standing up here and acting for you people who know nothing about actors, nothing about my art." Then he pulled out a gun and fired at the executives, full-load blanks.

He had trouble getting a job for years after that.

Dame Peggy Ashcroft

For many years, Dame Peggy was not only a distinguished Shakespearean interpreter and star of the London stage appearing with the likes of Gielgud, Richardson, and Olivier, but also was seen frequently in many quality films.

Well into her career, she was being seen by some casting person or producer and was asked, "What have you done?"

"You mean, this morning?" replied Dame Peggy.

Roscoe Lee Browne

At an audition for a play, the veteran actor was asked, "What have you done?"

"To whom?" Roscoe responded.

Larry Block

A long-time working character actor, Larry, auditioning for this relatively new director, was asked, "What have you done?"

Larry paused, then said, "You first."

Stephen Moorer

Auditioning for artistic director Moorer for his upcoming Shakespeare festival, an actress came out on stage to do her monologue holding a bowl of marbles in her hands. (Stephen swears it's true.) At the high point of her monologue, in dramatic fury, she spilled the bowl of marbles all over the floor of the stage . . . marbles were rolling everywhere.

Days after that audition, in various cracks and corners of the stage floor, marbles were found. To this day, Stephen cannot understand or explain why it all happened—unless, of course, the woman just . . . lost her marbles.

Peter Von Berg

l. Many years ago I booked a voiceover. They needed Russian speakers, and it's my native language. My manager called to say I had a booking. But they asked that I call them and give them the name of any other actors I might know, since they needed some more. I called and gave them my friend's name.

Days later I arrive at the studio to record. A woman comes out and says, "I'm sorry but we're going with your friend instead. Sorry. We should have called you earlier."

I never told my friend. I was too humiliated.

2. My friend Richard Thomas got me an audition for *Twelve Angry Men* for the Roundabout's national touring company. He was starring in it. It was for the role of the European immigrant. I worked like a banshee on it, got a friend to rehearse with me, the works. I read for it. There's a whole bunch of people sitting behind a table. The director, Scott Ellis, gets up, walks right up to me, shakes my hand, and says, "You nailed it."

You guessed it. Never heard from them again.

"Great! O.K., this time I want you to sound taller, and let me hear a little more hair."

Chapter Two
What??

Mel Gibson

Mel talks about his audition for the movie *Mad Max*:

"The night before I auditioned for it, I got mugged by three guys. They broke my nose, blackened my eyes. I had a slightly broken jaw but I could still talk. I was a mess. But I went to the audition anyway, and they loved the way I looked.

"I think without that beating I wouldn't have gotten the Max role."

Audrey Hepburn

In the early fifties in London, Roger Vadim was working as a screenwriter on a detective film, *Blackmail*. The director, Vadim's friend and mentor, was the noted Frenchman Marc Allégret. There was a supporting part in the film that had not been cast yet.

Allégret took Vadim to a private club to see the act of a young woman who opened the show dressed in a silver-sequined swimsuit, decorated with three ostrich feathers attached to the base of her spine. She was ravishing and she delivered her introduction with charm and humor. "She would be perfect for the part of Polly," Allégret told Vadim. For two weeks he fought to cast her in the part.

The producer wouldn't hear of it. "She's already done three screen tests," he said, "Nobody wants her. She has an impossible nose. There's no hope of a career for that girl."

"That girl" was Audrey Hepburn. The mistress of one of the film's backers got the part.

Paul Muni

Paul Muni began his career in his teens in the Yiddish Theatre of New York. His name then was Muni Weisenfreund, and like most young actors he played mainly old parts, while young romantic leads were the preserve of established actors pushing sixty. At the age of thirty-one, Muni had worked for eighteen years and played three hundred parts in Yiddish.

In October 1926, producer Sam Harris urgently needed a replacement for Edward G. Robinson, who was playing a very old man in a play called *We Americans*, by Herbert Gropper and Max Siegel.

Harris looked up at the youthful Muni when he walked in and dismissed him, saying, "Too young. He's just a kid." Muni turned to leave, but Siegel stopped him. Muni looked back at Harris, bent over, tottered toward Harris's desk. He wore no makeup, but his voice seemed as wise and ancient as time.

"Oh, sir, you're right. We old bastards shouldn't let any of these young punks into the theatre. What do they know—still wet in the diapers, still shitting in their pants?"

Harris laughed and looked over to the equally startled director, Forrest, who hadn't said a word, now said just two: "Sign him."

Dustin Hoffman

As young actors trying to get started in New York, Dustin and his roommate, Robert Duvall, got so tired of meeting and facing agents and being rejected that they would go to the office, slip their 8   10's under the door . . . and run like hell.

Pamela Payton-Wright

Pamela went to audition for the Broadway play *Jimmy Shine,* starring Dustin Hoffman. It was a year after *The Graduate,* which she hadn't seen. She didn't know him or who he was, but had a picture of what she imagined him to be: tall, blonde . . . a movie star. Pamela read the first scene with the stage manager, and then heard voices out there in the darkness. "Do you want her to read the next scene?"

"By all means," the director said.

They got to the next scene and the other stage manager came up on stage. They began to read. Pamela thought to herself: "He's a nebbishy guy, short, but he had *something.* The two of us together had sparks. If they were smart, this is who they should cast in the part, but of course, they get a movie star."

After Pamela auditioned, she went to her agent's office and told them what happened.

"You were reading with Dustin Hoffman," he told her.

George C. Scott

Zelda Fichandler recalls:

"In the fifties or sixties, actors were auditioning for me for the Arena Stage Company in D.C. In those days the theatre budget was overwhelmingly meager with no stage manager to handle the auditions. I did it all—answered the door and phone, set up chairs in the waiting room, filled out the postcards that scheduled the auditions—truly, a one-woman show. By the way, I used to get 1,000 resumes a year and see half that many people with a great sense of curiosity and adventure.

"So, one day this actor comes in, George C. Scott . . . probably before the plays with Colleen Dewhurst and Joe Papp in Central Park. (Otherwise, there's no excuse for me and I shouldn't be telling this story.)

"I don't remember his selections or my notes on his resume . . . but he was very withheld and I felt a frisson of fear generated by his inscrutability—or am I revising history? On my sheet was . . . 'wart on his nose' and 'unpleasant quality,' and thus George C. Scott never became a member of the Arena Stage Company. But managed to survive artistically at any rate."

Paul Scofield / David Selznick

Michael Powell, film director (*The Red Shoes*, *The Life and Death of Colonel Blimp*), was casting the movie *Gone to Earth*. One of the important roles in it was a Baptist minister. Powell liked Scofield for the part, and on the recommendation of the actress, Pamela Brown, a close friend of Powell's, decided to use him.

Wanting no squabbles or recriminatons from the producer, David Selznick, Powell left the final decision to him. At the screening, several other actors' tests were shown. Scofield's test was the last.

When the lights came up, there was a ten-second silence—then Selznick turned to Powell and in a low mysterious tone said, "Is he queer?"

Powell explained that Scofield was not only *not* queer, but was married to a beautiful actress and had children.

Selznick shook his head in disbelief . . . exit Paul.

The Beatles

When the Beatles were first starting out, they sent an audition tape to Decca records. The tape was returned with a note: "We don't like your sound. Besides guitar music is on the way out."

Allen Blumenfeld

A writer friend of Allen's wrote a screenplay with a part in it for Allen; in fact, it *was* Allen—he would essentially be playing himself. You know the story: Allen went to the audition and was told that he wasn't right for it.

David Mamet

Newly arrived in New York, David went to an agent's office looking for representation.

Agent: "So what have you done?"

David: "*Sexual Perversity in Chicago.*"

Agent: "What have you done in New York?"

Alex Rocco

Rocco, auditioning for the movie *The Godfather,* was told to read the Mario Puzo book and pick the role he wanted to read for. He chose a rather small part. He went to see Francis Ford Coppola, who immediately took one look at Rocco and said, "Moe Greene! You're Moe Greene!" This was *not* the part that Rocco chose.

Rocco said, "But Mr. Coppola, I'm Italian. Moe Greene is Jewish. I wouldn't know how to play a Jew!"

Coppola replied, "Mr. Rocco, the only difference is, an Italian does this with his hands" (demonstrating: thumb touching forefinger and the middle finger—moving both hands in front of him), "a Jew opens his hands, and spreads his arms."

Mr. Rocco was handed the part.

Spalding Gray

Known for many years primarily as a monologist performing his own works, Spalding said, "Part of me wants to go back and show people in the commercial world of theatre and film that I can play a character. It's good for me to read for things, because I've lost the knack of auditioning. Competition is very threatening to me—that's why I went into my own work.

"When I went to Los Angeles to audition for *Hail to the Chief* with Patty Duke, it was just between Dick Shawn and me. They were auditioning in a good-sized room, like a little theatre, and all the producers were sitting in the dark. They pulled me down too early, so I was sitting outside the door for Shawn's audition and it made me so fucking self-conscious. First of all, they were laughing a lot, then I had to get his line readings out of my head and try to do something different. The problem is, you want to bring nuance to lines like, 'I can't do it with you anymore. How can I make love to the President of the United States—you're my commander-in-chief!'"

Spalding was not heartbroken when he didn't get the part. He didn't expect to get it. He continued with his monologues, of which he was his own commander-in-chief.

Lew Wasserman

Lew, head of the giant talent agency in Hollywood, M.C.A., met Grace Kelly when she was eighteen: "The most beautiful thing I've ever seen." He told M.C.A.'s head theatrical agent, Edith Van Cleve, to put her in a play.

"What can she do?" Van Cleve wanted to know.

"She can't *do* anything, I just want her to walk across the stage!" Wasserman said.

They put her in a play, Stanley Kramer saw her, and he hired her for *High Noon*, opposite Gary Cooper.

Ray Walston

1. After making a good impression in a few plays on Broadway, Ray was sent up for the musical *South Pacific*. With Richard Rodgers, Oscar Hammerstein II, and director Josh Logan sitting in, he was asked to sing something.

Ray: "I didn't know I was supposed to."

Richard: "Well, can you sing anything?"

Ray: "I don't know anything."

Richard: "Can you sing 'My Country 'tis of Thee'?"

Ray nodded and sang it.

Richard: "I've never heard it sung so funny."

Ray went on to play Luther Billis in *South Pacific* for four years.

2. Out in Hollywood, Ray had gone to see Billy Wilder, who was directing the movie *The Apartment*.

Billy: "Josh Logan tells me you're a very good actor."

Ray nodded.

Billy: "Do you have an overcoat?"

Ray nodded.

Billy: "Is it an expensive overcoat?"

Ray nodded.

Billy: "You've got the part."

3. Though he had great success on TV in *My Favorite Martian* and in many movies in Hollywood, Ray still had to audition for the judge on David Kelley's TV series *Picket Fences*. The audition was held before a number of network executives. And David, among others.

Ray was angry when he came in. As he read, he was angry and when he finished, he threw the script on the floor, walked out, and slammed the door behind him.

Kelley knew he had his judge.

Lehman Engel

Lehman, at the time one of the best musical conductors on the Broadway scene and author of books on the musical theatre, got a phone call from someone high up in his agency (one of the top-ranked agencies) asking Lehman to have lunch with him. Lehman met with the man, who began to tell him how much he admired and respected his work and how he would like to work with him.

Lehman looked at the man straight in the eye and quietly said, "I've been with you for four years."

Ron McLarty

Ron, a veteran of a number of TV series (*Spenser for Hire*, *The Longest Running One*), was flown out to Los Angeles to audition for a new TV pilot. A limo picked him up at the airport, took him to his hotel, and then to the NBC studios in Burbank to face the network executives.

He read one scene, then another. They talked . . . he was asked to read another scene. They thanked him for coming in to audition. Ron felt pretty good about it all, until he went out of the building, finding no limo, but a taxi to take him back to his hotel.

He, naturally, did not have a good feeling about this. Several days later, his agent called . . . he didn't get the part. Ron, puzzled, says, "But I was in there for more than an hour."

"Ron, they loved you . . . but they hated your work."

Richard Pryor

Richard first went to Hollywood to get into movies and be a star. "I knowed I was a star. Natural born. 'Cause I couldn't do nothin' else. So I went to this audition. Mother f—er said it was for *King Kong*. He gave me the script. I didn't know what the story was. *King Kong*. I said, I don't mind being a king. Sh—. That's a pretty good part. Change the mother f—er's last name, you know, to Williams or somebody. A little too Chinese for me, that Kong sh—.

"The director said, 'I don't believe you understand . . . this is a movie about a gorilla.' I replied, 'Well, you got the wrong nigger, mother f—er I ain't no mother f—ing gorilla. And I don't appreciate you callin' me into this audition.' I took the script and threw the mother f—er down. Them mother f—ers had me out of there so fast.

"I got on a freight train and went all the way home."

Noel Coward

Bea Lillie, working in London with Andre Charlot, was asked by her friend, young Noel Coward, for an introduction to Mr. Charlot, one of the more prestigious producers of the time.

"Noel was then rather condescending, paper thin, with a faint lisp. He was already writing songs, songs with a difference. Instead of moonlight and roses, there was a dash of vinegar . . . he was very clever but uncomfortable to be with at times."

Rehearsing a new revue, Bea "knew Charlot would be there . . . so I told my ambitious young friend, 'Just come up and be ready to audition.' Charlot gave me a filthy look when I introduced this nervous young man. 'I just want him to play this song he's written, 'Forbidden Fruit.'

"Though listening politely, Charlot could scarcely wait for him to finish. He shook his hand, walked him to the door, 'Very kind of you, thank you very much.' He just stopped short of slamming the door behind him. 'How dare you,' he said, turning on me, 'bring people here with no talent *whatsoever!*'"

James Komack

James's friend Jackie Cooper, directing the TV series *Hennesey*, needed a thin, good-looking actor for the part of a navy dentist. At breakfast with publicist Marilyn Reiss, Jackie told her his casting problem. "Get Komack," she said. Jackie said he was not right physically. "Have you seen him lately? He's lost weight, he's tanned, etc." That wasn't the Komack Jackie knew from dinners at his house.

But he sees Komack, works hard with him. The producer has Komack read for him three different times and for some reason is not sold on him.

At the last reading, Jackie, on a hunch, standing behind Komack, flattens Komack's protruding ears. "That's it!!" The producer says, "That's the guy, the ears!! If you were rich, your parents would have had your ears fixed!!"

Margaret Whitton

Whitton tells this story:

The king of spaghetti westerns was making an epic about the American dream, *Once Upon a Time in America*, starring Robert De Niro and James Woods. I got the call from my agent because they wanted a "period face," a concept that eludes me to this day. "Don't be surprised if he doesn't talk to you . . . that means he likes you," I was told by his assistant.

I walked in and was introduced to a very large man in a smallish chair. He flicked his wrist at me, a sign that I was to begin. I read nearly everything in the script, my excitement rising with every nod to continue. No words. I read brilliantly. He kept nodding and waving his hand imperiously, scene after scene. "He must *really* really like me," I thought.

My heart was racing, along with my mind (it was pretty thin material) we read on. Finally he held his hand up and spoke to me, "You have extraordinary face . . . there is no room in my movie for this face . . . goodbye."

Jack Warden

Jack, a discharged World War II paratrooper, worked in a garage while studying acting. He went to see John Houseman, directing *King Lear*, straight from his job, having no time to change his greasy coveralls.

Houseman looked at Jack contemptuously. "What part do you see yourself playing?" Jack, with no chance in hell to be cast, said, "Well, shit, who's doin' Lear?"

Tony Lo Bianco

Rocky Marciano was one of the greatest heavyweight boxing champions of his day, and when it was announced that a movie of the week was to be made of his life for TV, the noted actor Mr. Lo Bianco instantly felt it was a role made to order for him. He called his agent for an audition, got it, and read, but was told he wasn't right for the part. That only made Tony more determined. He went to work. He did his research, studied pictures, got film on Rocky, went to a make-up artist to get the look right: the hair, the broken nose. He worked on Rocky's moves.

Another audition was arranged. Other actors went before him, then it was Tony's turn. The very same producers who rejected him the first time, sat up, "My God! That's him! That actor . . . that *is* Marciano! Who is he?"

Gary Merrill

Film director Otto Preminger was working on the film *Where the Sidewalk Ends*. Gary was up for the part of a sharply dressed gangster and was cast. Hours were spent picking the right clothes for him, but something was gnawing at Gary. He just did not feel right as a gangster.

After much personal distress, Gary, aware of Otto's reputation bordering on tyrannical, finally steeled himself to talk to Otto about it. He went to Otto's hotel where Otto was shaving . . . in the bathtub.

"Otto, this part is not me, I don't know him. I simply cannot do it."

The lathered Otto looked at him and said, "Don't tell me, tell your psychiatrist."

Charlton Heston

Gerald Hiken heard Mr. Heston was going to do *A Man for All Seasons*, a play that Gerry adored. He called everyone he knew, desperate to be in it. It paid off. He got an audition. Before going, without realizing what he was taking, he had a "Thai stick," a marijuana-like substance that someone offered him.

The after-effects were awful. He didn't know where he was or what he was doing. He wandered around lost . . . until he saw a sign on a building: "Theatre." He went in and was greeted by the assistant who said, "You're early, Mr. Hiken." Then he realized where he was and why.

He read with Mr. Heston and was cast as Everyman. After the run, Mr. Heston told him why he got the part. "It wasn't that you were good or bad, but you showed me how you work, not what you were going to do with the part—and I have never had the guts to do that."

Dorothy Dandridge

Producer/director Otto Preminger was seeing stars and big movie names for his film *Carmen Jones*, the all-black version of Bizet's opera *Carmen*, and particularly he was looking for someone to play the lead . . . the seductive gypsy woman.

Carmen Jones had been a big hit in New York on stage, but Mr. Preminger, following the standard Hollywood practice in adapting it for the movies, had no intention of using the original leads from the Broadway show.

Mr. Preminger saw Dorothy for the lead, Carmen, but turned her down, saying, "She has too much class for the part." But Dorothy would not give up. She demanded another audition and got it. She had told a friend she would get the part . . . and she did.

According to Dorothy, it was because of the dirty underwear she wore to the audition.

Jon Voight

Early in his career as an actor in New York, Jon found himself auditioning for the hit musical *The Sound of Music*, by Rodgers and Hammerstein. It was for a replacement, and Jon, not primarily a singer, but feeling in fairly good voice that day, gave it a go.

He sang, said, "Thank you," and as he was leaving his manager hurried up to him and said, "Jon, where are you going? They want you."

Jon, shocked, said, "What?"

"Richard Rodgers is out there and he wants you."

"But tell him I can't sing!" Jon said.

The Sound of Music was Jon Voight's first Broadway show.

Robert De Niro

Alan Willig, an agent for twenty years, originally began in the theatre as an actor and naturally went through all the rigors and absurdities of the audition process. Early on, he got to be friends with another young and inexperienced actor named Robert De Niro. Both he and Bobby found themselves frequently at the same auditions and inevitably with the same result—nothing. In fact, they joked that if they both were auditioning for the same part, it was a guarantee that neither one would get the job.

One day at an audition, Alan noticed Bobby carrying a huge portfolio, the kind that commercial artists use to carry their drawings. Puzzled, Alan asked him why. Bobby explained that he had all his clippings and photos of himself in plays he had appeared in since grammar school, high school, and so on.

"I once played Peter Rabbit in school, and I played . . ."

"Bobby, listen to me, no one gives a damn about those reviews and stuff. Trust me."

"Alan, you never know . . . you never know."

Woody Allen

Starting out as a comedy writer, Woody looked much younger than he really was. Woody's humor sometimes got him into trouble. Particularly with people who had no sense of humor. One of them was Max Liebman, the powerful producer of many of the early television comedy shows. When Woody was summoned to his first interview, he could barely see Liebman behind his huge desk, which was covered with three dozen awards, ranging from Emmys to Peabodys. Woody looked at the forest of statuettes and said, "Gee, Max, I didn't know you played tennis." It was the end of the interview.

Larry Bryggman

Bryggman recalls:

I have never thought anything funny about auditions— they scare the hell out of me, and I am convinced that I don't know how to do them.

John McTiernan hired me to be in *Die Hard with a Vengeance*. I had auditioned on tape in New York with the casting director, then the tape was sent to California for McTiernan to look at. Weeks went by. Then one day my agent called saying I had the job.

One day well into the shoot, I finally asked him what was on the tape that got me the job. He looked at me and said, "You looked like you had a headache."

Charles Bronson

Bronson appeared in a number of very successful films in Europe, but it wasn't until his movie *Death Wish* came out and became a big hit that established Bronson as a star.

Bronson, while taking classes at the Pasadena Playhouse, earned a little money at odd jobs, like selling Christmas cards and toys on street corners. He got a break in a movie, *You're in the Navy Now* starring Gary Cooper, a minor role, because he was the only one among all the auditioning actors who could belch on cue.

Jane Curtin

TV producer Lorne Michaels came up with a fresh idea for a show: a live sketch-comedy format using performers with improvisational theatre backgrounds. Among the many people auditioning was blonde, petite Jane Curtin, who, with actress friend Judy Kahn, presented a situation involving two wives from the heartland wondering how to cope with the annual tornado (including lines such as "Can I borrow your centerpiece for the tornado this year?").

Another actress to audition was Mimi Kennedy, whose choice was a song "I Am Dog." If it has a familiar ring, it was a take-off of "I Am Woman" by Helen Reddy.

It came down to Jane or Mimi. The producers were leaning towards Mimi, but Dick Ebersole, the head honcho, went with Jane. Why? Two actresses already chosen, Gilda Radner and Laraine Newman, had different qualities—quirkier maybe, more off-the-wall than conventional "white-bread"

Jane Curtin. There were more comic possibilities and variety with opposites, he figured.

The lesson here: it's not always talent that wins out, but sometimes balance.

Sam Spiegel

1. Homosexuality, cannibalism, insanity, and a lobotomy— elements in *Suddenly Last Summer*, a play by Tennessee Williams—did not, to Sam, seem to be a problem in converting it into a movie. Sam had other worries, namely: paying Liz Taylor the most money ever to a screen actress, half-a-million dollars, to star in it and then fighting with her over her choice of a leading man, Montgomery Clift, who during filming was going through tremendous personal problems and struggles. She also had her choice of directors, Joe Mankiewicz, who sided with Liz in disputes with Sam.

After viewing the dailies on Clift, Sam felt they were so bad, he wanted to replace him, but Liz's reaction was a resounding *no!*

Behind their backs, Sam set up a screen test with Peter O'Toole playing a doctor operating on a patient. At the finish, O'Toole, known for his outrageous behavior, looked dead-on into the camera and Sam and ad-libbed, "It's all right, Mrs. Spiegel, your son will never play the violin again."

Sam erupted, vowing that O'Toole would never work with him . . . 'til *Lawrence of Arabia*. Clift finished the picture.

2. Once Sam got the rights for *Lawrence of Arabia* and his director, David Lean, he went through a few writers before he got the right one, Robert Bolt (*A Man for All Seasons*).

Finding the perfect Lawrence, the title role, was not as easy. Among those considered, at one time or another for some reason or other, were Marlon Brando, Anthony Perkins, Alec Guinness, and Albert Finney.

The next actor to be screen-tested was Peter O'Toole. Now Sam had a run-in with O'Toole when he tested him for *Suddenly Last Summer*; at that time, he swore that he would never, ever work with the free-spirited, larger-than-life O'Toole.

Sam put him through the wringer, insisting O'Toole test in full Arab regalia. Apparently, O'Toole was utterly convincing. Sam offered him the role, at which point, O'Toole blithely asked, "Is it a speaking part?"

Ethan Phillips

Ethan, looking for someone to represent him, went to an agent a friend had recommended. He walked into the office and upon seeing him, the agent, assuming he looked familiar, said, "You . . . you are wonderful! Just . . . just terrific! And . . . and funny, really funny. . . . Aaah . . . what have you done?"

Walter Beakel

As a young actor in New York City, Walter auditioned for a play he loved a lot, Strindberg's *Miss Julie*. He was told then and there that the part was his. He never went back. He felt anyone who was dumb enough to hire him had to have something wrong with him.

William Duell

Duell played the character Filch for six years in the off-Broadway hit *Three Penny Opera*. It featured such performers as Lotte Lenya, Bea Arthur, Ed Asner, Paul Dooley, Joe Elic, and Jerry Orbach. Years later, it was revived. Up for Filch, he was told he wasn't right for it.

Morley Safer

Morley, one of the current correspondents on CBS's *60 Minutes*, once was a London-based reporter for the Canadian Broadcasting Company when the network's anchorman, Stanley Burke, decided, as so many other Canadians have done, to apply for a higher-paying job in American television.

As a sample of his work, Burke sent to CBS News a tape of a year-end roundtable discussion by various CBC correspondents. The people at CBS News were more impressed by Morley Safer, and sent him an unsolicited job offer from New York.

Faith Prince

As a struggling singer/actress in New York, Faith felt things wouldn't come to her if she stayed quiet. She had a girlfriend, a beautiful girl, who could just sit there, not say a word, and people would come to her. That didn't work for Faith, she realized she wasn't getting what she needed, so she decided to speak up.

With her mother, she went down to the village to see a friend performing in *Scrambled Feet*. At the intermission, her mother said that Faith would be very good in the show. Faith listened and at the question-and-answer session after the show, Faith raised her hand and said, "I have just one question, do you need another girl?" They did; she auditioned and got the part.

Anonymous

Director: "Could you stand back a little?"
Actor: "Is this far enough?"
Director: "Further."
Actor: "How about this?"
Director: "Further."

Actor: "How far should I go?"
Director: "Do you have a car?"

Marsha Mason

After a season of doing plays with ACT (American Conservatory Theatre) in San Francisco, Marsha's agent called about reading for the new Neil Simon play *The Good Doctor* in New York.

"But I want to go back to ACT next season; I love repertory."

"And you probably will go back, but it's important to audition for Neil and his producer Manny Azenberg."

She auditioned with a scene she had worked on without a worry or care, figuring she already had a job waiting for her in San Francisco. They then asked her to read the next scene.

"I was only given one scene." But feeling no fear and full of confidence, she said, "I'll read it cold . . . I'll go for broke."

After reading it, Neil Simon turned to Manny Azenberg and said, "Hire that girl, I'm going to marry her."

Rehearsals started October 3, 1973, and on October 25 Neil Simon and Marsha Mason were married.

Armin Shimerman

Shimerman tells this story:

Having been seduced by the dark side of the force to move to Los Angeles from New York, I spent my first year desperately trying to get my foot in the studio door. The most memorable audition was for a casting director, whose name I've long since forgotten, who called me in for some minuscule role she was casting. I suppose when I walked into the office, she decided in her mind I was not physically "right." I'll never forget her response to my theatre-oriented resume. "Oh, you're an actor. We don't need an actor, we just need someone to do this part."

Philip Seymour Hoffman

Philip, who in the last few years has been prominently featured and critically acclaimed in a number of movies such as *Boogie Nights, Happiness, Magnolia,* and *The Talented Mr. Ripley,* went to his first audition when he was fifteen years old.

Because he was hungry and passionate about the theatre? No, he went to the audition to chase a girl named Amy . . . who was actually going after his older brother!

Roddy McDowell

McDowell tells this story:

A little girl, only four years old, came to an audition with her mother. The shy, pretty four-year-old was hanging back but her mother was pushing her forward. The director interviewing her asked the little four-year-old why she wanted to be an actress.

The child hesitated, so the mother jumped in and said, "Oh, it's been her life-long dream."

Kim Hunter

When asked for any memorable audition stories in her long and distinguished career, Kim, the original Stella in the stage and screen versions of *A Streetcar Named Desire,* said she had none. None?

None. Once the audition is over Kim doesn't remember anything.

Kim Stanley

1. Kim, when a young actress, never felt herself pretty enough to be in movies, but plays to her were more "about something." So she headed for New York City. She didn't know anything or anybody, but she had absolute confidence in herself. It didn't occur to her that they wouldn't give her a job.

She went up to Kermit Bloomgarden's office, straight off the bus, and told him he would have to replace Barbara Bel Geddes in *Deep Are the Roots* because she, Kim, was right for the part because, coming from the South, she knew more about it.

From the yellow pages, she got the names of all the theatrical producers and saw them all just this way. She didn't know that she had to please the secretary first. She saw the door where someone walked in, and she'd just walk in and do her pieces from *St. Joan* and *Juliet*.

They were stunned or they would have thrown her out.

"I never got a job from it. You just don't *do* that. Walk in like that, unannounced . . . except in the movies."

2. John Bacher wanted very much to study with the renowned actress Ms. Stanley, who was teaching acting, but in order to get into her one of her classes John was required to audition for Ms. Stanley herself.

At the audition, John was asked by Ms. Stanley to act out: the time of day, the temperature, and the specific time of the year . . . without using any words.

John turned around and walked out of the room.

Brenda Fricker

The first time Brenda auditioned for the British director Alan Parker, she did very badly. Mr. Parker said, "You will never make it in this business."

Later in her career she again auditioned for a part for Mr. Parker, and Mr. Parker said, "You'll never work with me."

When Brenda won an Oscar as Best Supporting Actress in the movie *My Left Foot*, playing Daniel Day-Lewis's mother,

Mr. Parker approached her, got on his knees before her as though she were a queen and said, "I was wrong . . . you are great!"

Anonymous

This first-time film director, who said he had some names attached to the project, called me in to read. The scene had two characters. I was ushered into the room where the director was seated behind a desk. He offered me a seat and asked me to start reading. I read my first line. Nobody answered.

"Excuse me, isn't there another actor in the scene?" I asked.

"He had to leave. It's okay. Read your lines, then act like you're hearing his lines, then you say your lines, okay? . . . Hey, where are you going?"

"*I* have to leave!" . . . and he left.

Karl Malden

"I never got a part that I auditioned for."

Rudolph Valentino

At the peak of his career, from his tantalizing tango in *The Four Horsemen of the Apocalypse* to *The Sheik*, Valentino became the sex symbol of his era, driving both young and old women wild, long before the Beatles and Presley came along.

Ironically, Valentino was up for a part in a movie directed by the giant of silent films, D. W. Griffith, who rejected him, saying "The girls will never like him . . . too foreign-looking."

Hume Cronyn

The late Hume Cronyn, veteran of stage plays ranging from Shakespeare to Beckett, and films from Spencer Tracy to Hitchcock, had a very inauspicious start as an actor. Many years ago, searching for work in New York, Cronyn was advised by the casting director of the Theatre Guild to go into summer stock and she told him, "You may have a difficult time because you don't look like anything."

Reviewing *Triple Play* for the *New York Times* in 1959, drama critic Brooks Atkinson said, "Give a wig, mustache and glasses to Mr. Cronyn, and he is about the best character actor in the business."

Louis Zorich

In the seventies, New York was the busiest producer of TV commercials. I frequently had three or more auditions a day, on camera and voice-overs. One morning I read for two voice-overs, one for a car, the other a cereal. I hadn't been getting many voice-overs at the time, so when my agent called to tell me I had a booking I was more than surprised.

"The car one?" I asked, because I gave a great audition. "No, the cereal one." That was odd. That audition I thought I sucked, but what the hell, I took it, voice-overs were hard to get.

At the recording session on the third take, I began to feel what I was doing was awful, I mean, awful. Unable to contain myself, I asked the producer, "Why did you hire me, I'm terrible."

"I know," he said.

"What? Then why did you hire me?"

"Because when you auditioned, you gave the worst reading."

Shocked, I said, "But if I was so bad . . . I don't understand?"

The producer said, "That's what we wanted . . . someone who did it very badly, you were the best one."

Marlene Dietrich

In the twenties and thirties, Germany's film capital was Berlin. Rudolf Seiber worked as an assistant to the young director Alexander Korda. One day he asked Korda if his wife might get the tiniest part in their current film. Korda told him that the lady had not the slightest potential as a film actress.

That lady, Frau Seiber, later became much better known as Marlene Dietrich.

Malcolm Black

1. Black tells this story:

As director, I was auditioning actors for the play *Gaslight* at the Walnut Theatre in Philadelphia. A young man came in who was much too young for either of the male leads but I said we needed two young cops for the fight scene. He immediately said, "I'll give you a 'physical monologue.'" A physical monologue . . . ? Ok.

He did! A kung fu-type demonstration that was fascinating and a first for me. He got the job.

2. I hate auditions. I remember years ago as an actor in London waiting my turn along with the other actors and hearing a young man crucifying the start of the song "Some Enchanted Evening." Very early on they stopped him with "Thank you . . . we'll call you."

The young man replied, "Wait, hold on, I haven't got a phone."

The producer responded angrily, "I said . . . we'd call you!"

George Sperdakos

Being seen for a role, George was told he wasn't right because he was bald. George promptly replied, "I can *act* hair!!"

Carol Teitel

Her agent at the time, Lillian Arnold, called Carol to go out on an audition for the part of a fat woman.

Carol: "But I'm ninety-eight pounds. Skinny!"

Lillian: "What is this actor's studio stuff? Put on a shawl, puff up your cheeks and go!"

Michael O'Sullivan

Michael, auditioning for the Broadway musical *Superman*, was given sides to read on stage before the producers and creative people. He took the sides and proceeded very slowly to tear them up, saying, "I do not read," and walked off . . . he got the part.

"I got another callback. My agent says it's between me and the guy who's going to get it."

Chapter Three

Get the Job

Madonna

Mike Medavoy in his memoirs tells this one on Madonna:

Based on the success of Susan Seidelman's first film, *Smithereens*, we picked up *Desperately Seeking Susan*. Susan was a bohemian commercial director with no track record. Unable to get Ellen Barkin to star with Rosanna Arquette, she held a casting call for some two hundred actresses in New York to find the right Susan.

The character was written as an old soul who happens to be charmingly promiscuous. After a tireless auditioning process, Susan settled on a little-known pop singer with a stage name Madonna. She had never been in a film.

Barbara Boyle, my head of production, told Susan that Madonna would have to shoot an audition tape to be shown to my partners and me for approval. She had one album out in record stores that wasn't selling well. Neither Barbara nor I had heard of her but Barbara's fifteen-year-old had—a good sign in respect to attracting a teenage audience. Before the audition tape was made, Susan encouraged Barbara to meet Madonna face-to-face.

One afternoon, Madonna appeared in Barbara's office wearing a second-hand miniskirt over thick leggings, rhinestone boots, and plastic bracelets on her wrists. Madonna instantly sank to her knees, stretched out her arms, bowed dramatically, and purred to Barbara in her sexiest voice, "I'll do anything to get this role."

"I'm married and I'm straight," Barbara responded.

"Well, Barbara," Madonna retorted, "you should try everything at least once."

William H. Macy

Macy's biggest, or at least longest, audition was for Joel and Ethan Coen, directors of the movie *Fargo*. He was called in to read for one of the smaller parts, which he did. They said, "That's real good. You want to read for Jerry Lundegaard?"

"Yeah, I'd love to," he said. He went out in the hall, worked on it for five minutes, came back and read it.

"That's real good. You want to go home and work on it and come back tomorrow?"

He agreed.

So every actor Macy knew in Los Angeles was up all night with him. He ran the scenes until he was sick of them. He auditioned the next day.

"That was really good. You want to do anything else?"

He said, "No that's it. Just give me the role."

They said, "Yeah, well, we'll call you."

Then he found out later they were still auditioning actors . . . in New York! Macy caught a plane to New York, walked in and said, "I want to audition again . . . and if you don't give me this role I'll kill your dog."

Macy was nominated for Best Supporting Actor for his role, Jerry Lundegaard, in the film *Fargo*.

Rosie O'Donnell

O'Donnell tells this story:

I wish I could say it was after years of tap dancing classes, hours and hours of vocal training, and many day jobs . . .

but the truth is—I did a lot of movies. Broadway was always a dream of mine. A mecca for the best in the business.

After my big-time Hollywood agent got done screaming at me and calling me insane, she reluctantly booked an audition for the Broadway revival of the musical *Grease*. I walked onto the empty stage of a Broadway theatre, and feeling very much like Fanny Brice, called out to the producers in the darkness: "Hey listen, I can't really sing and dance, but I'll sell a lot of tickets!"

Those producers, Barry and Fran Weissler, who I would later come to affectionately call "the cheapest people on Broadway," recognized my particular talent . . . and got me my Equity card.

Gregory Peck

Gregory has related this story frequently in various interviews. In the late forties, Gregory was an unknown actor appearing in a Neighborhood Playhouse production at the Heckscher Theatre on Forty-Sixth Street near Fifth Avenue. One day he happened to be in the Playhouse's fourth floor offices when the phone rang.

He overheard the secretary on the phone talking to Guthrie McClintock. It seems that he had seen Gregory's show the night before and he wanted to see this actor named Gregory Peck for a new production of *The Doctor's Dilemma* that he was going to direct starring his wife, the then-reigning first lady of the American theatre, Katharine Cornell.

Peck dashed out of the door, ran down four flights of stairs, from Fifth Avenue to Sixth Avenue, up Sixth Avenue to the RKO Building on Fiftieth Street, and up to McClintock's office on the tenth floor. As he ran in the door, McClintock was still on the phone with the secretary of the Neighborhood Playhouse. He looked up in amazement and said, "He's here." The out-of-breath Gregory Peck got the job.

Oprah Winfrey

Oprah was auditioning for a small local Chicago-based TV talk show. Not the typical slim, white blonde, Oprah had some misgivings. Luckily, the general manager, Dennis Swanson, saw Oprah as a woman who had a gift for really connecting with people, an intuitive sense of sharing of herself. "Be yourself," he said simply, which led to what has become today as the Oprah Winfrey phenomenon.

Jerry Stiller

"They're looking for someone short, a short pirate who can sing and dance for the national company of *Peter Pan*," an actor friend told Jerry, "The Majestic Theatre, hurry!"

Jerry rushed over, but the casting call was over. He told the stage manager, "I don't have an appointment, but can you squeeze me in? I'm funny."

SM: "Do you sing?"

Jerry: "Kinda."

SM: "Do you dance?"

Jerry: "A little."

SM: "Well, you've got to do both."

Jerry: "Let me audition . . . I won't disappoint you."

Though they were all set with the casting, they agreed to see Jerry. He auditioned with his version of an Italian soap opera singing "Sorrento." They were laughing. Afterward, the director, Frank Corsaro, came up on stage and said, "We know you can't sing and you probably can't dance, but you're funny and we do need one more pirate. We have something of a problem here. The guy who originally did the show on Broadway hasn't made up his mind about going out on the road. If he says no, then the job is yours."

Jerry: "When will you know?"

Director: "Well, right now he's singing in the chorus at the Roxy. Why don't you go there and ask him?"

Jerry ran down to the Roxy stage entrance and waited for the actor to come out. When he emerged, Jerry, breathless and excited, explained the situation to the actor, then asked, "Are you going to stay with this show or are you going out with *Peter Pan?*"

After what seemed an eternity to Jerry, the actor said, "I told them I wouldn't go on the road unless they hired my wife . . . well, you've got the part."

Peter Sellers

The place was London, the time, 1948. After some unsuccessful auditions for BBC radio variety, Sellers, with his many voices and comedy impressions, resorted to a caper he later recounted many times.

Roy Speer was a BBC radio producer of *Show Time*, a show that had lots of new acts, and Peter had written in many times to get on it, with no reply. Peter, with the feeling of "You've got to get ahead, you've got to get ahead!" knew that one of the big shows on the air featured Kenneth Horne and Dickie Murdock, and Roy Speer being an executive producer, would probably know them . . . "If I click with the secretary, I'll get out through."

So I phoned: "Oh hello, I'm Ken Horne, is Roy there?"

"Oh," she says, "yes he is" and I knew I was all right.

So Roy got on and said "Hello, Ken, how are you?"

I said, "Listen Roy, I'm calling because I know that new show you got on—what is it? *Show Time* or something?— Dickie and I were at the cabaret the other night, saw an amazing young fellow called Peter, what was his name? . . . Sellers . . . Peter Sellers, and he was very good you know.

Probably have him on the show you know, just thought I'd give you a little tip . . . a little tip."

Speer said, "Well that's very nice of you." Then I said, "It's me." He said, "What?" "It's me, Peter Sellers talking . . . it's the only way I could get to you and will you give me a date on the show?"

He said, "What do you do?"

I said, "Well, obviously, impersonations."

Peter had a booking at last.

James Caan

Director Rob Reiner worked on the Stephen King script *Misery* for months with Warren Beatty before Warren walked away from playing the lead role, Paul Sheldon, a writer.

Among the other top name actors who turned it down were Harrison Ford, Michael Douglas, Dustin Hoffman, Robert De Niro, Gene Hackman, Kevin Kline, Richard Dreyfuss, and William Hurt.

Reiner then went to James Caan, but Caan had a history of substance abuse and consequent reputation as being difficult. Desperate to work again, Caan assured Reiner, "I'll pee in a bottle for you. I will pee in a bottle every day." Caan got the part and gave a sterling performance.

Richard Harris

Richard (*Sporting Life, A Man Called Horse, Camelot*) heard about a film being cast that he felt he was supremely right for, but he couldn't get to the producer for whatever reason. His agent was no help. Harris tried calling the producer, he sent wires, he wrote letters, nothing worked. Not one to give up too easily, Harris somehow learned that the producer was having lunch at one of Hollywood's trendier restaurants. He schemed to make a deal with one of the waiters, got into the waiter's jacket and approached the producer's table with a menu and his order pad.

Not paying any particular attention to his waiter, the producer scanning the menu was suddenly aware of the waiter's face bending over him pointing out the day's specials. He turned up to recognize Harris, who introduced himself and began to tell him why he should play that part. Harris, hard to ignore, finally convinced him. He got the part—and he took his order.

Charlize Theron

Charlize arrived in Los Angeles in 1994 with dreams of becoming an actress, very little dramatic training and "a couple of hundred bucks in my bag," she recalls, "but I was completely fearless."

That fearlessness served her well. When director John Herzfeld was auditioning actresses for the movie *2 Days*, he asked them to *sit* and read a scene in which the role of Helga was shot and killed.

But Charlize *unexpectedly* fell to the floor and crawled across the room as she read her lines; when she died, a star was born.

Whoopi Goldberg

Coming off of an Academy Award nomination for *The Color Purple*, Whoopi began to catch on to finding out what projects were coming up and what roles she might go after. She heard about a Rob Reiner movie, *The Princess Bride*. Idealistic and rather naïve about the politics of moviemaking, Whoopi wanted to audition for the part of Buttercup, the princess bride, even though it was conceived as a blonde, fair-complexioned beautiful maiden. She thought if she wished and tried hard enough, she could convince the studio heads to cast her against type in such a part.

Rob Reiner, the director, got a call.

Agent: "You still haven't got a Buttercup?"

Reiner: "Have you got one?"

Agent: "It's amazing casting!"

Reiner (growing impatient): "I'm waiting. I'm waiting."

Agent: "Whoopi Goldberg!"

Reiner ended the phone call as a very bad joke. The call was from Whoopi posing as an agent.

Howie Mandel

Around 1979, Howie came to Los Angeles from Canada to become a stand-up comic. He knocked around the club circuit, but the holy grail was to get on Johnny Carson's *The Tonight Show*. His talent bookers regularly scouted the comedy club, and it was there that Howie was told not only was he wrong for their show, but that he would *never* be on it.

Luckily, Howie was a regular on the hit drama series *St. Elsewhere* as a serious actor, but it hurt him to see all his comedy club friends on the Carson show. He felt a failure.

One night in 1984, he heard Joan Rivers was looking for talent at the comedy store. She was the exclusive guest host of *The Tonight Show*, Johnny's hand-picked sub. Howie made sure that he was booked that night at the club.

That morning, Howie woke up with the worst flu of his life . . . 104-degree fever, chills, horrible nausea . . . literally delirious. "I could not let this chance pass me by . . . I climbed out of my deathbed and summoned every ounce of energy I had to drive down to the club . . . I'm shivering, I can barely grip the steering wheel . . . trembling like an epileptic. I didn't care, even if I fainted on stage, I had to try. This might be my last shot."

There he was, waiting almost three hours to go on, leaning against the railing . . . to keep from collapsing. Finally:

"Ladies and gentlemen . . . a warm welcome for Mr. Howie Mandel!"

Bam! The adrenaline kicks in. He got his second wind from nowhere that carries him through. Everyone's laughing, including Joan. He stumbles off stage and waits at the bottom of the stairs, struggling to catch his breath. And there's Joan, right there!

"What's your name?"

"Howie Mandel," gasping.

"You're very funny . . . have you ever been on *The Tonight Show?* Why don't you come on when I host next week?"

He did . . . and twenty-one times with Johnny Carson.

Danny Aiello

This is David Orange's story about Danny and David and a play called *Knockout.* Naturally, it's about boxing, and they were seeing boxers who couldn't act and actors who couldn't box. David could do both, but he was unable to see Danny to audition.

He heard that Danny hung out with his pals at a certain bar. Strangely enough, that night, the then–Cassius Clay was fighting on TV and doing his thing, "I am the greatest. . . ." Inspired by this, David felt courageous enough to go to the bar and confront Danny.

He was in a corner with his drinking buddies when David walked up to him and said, "You don't know me, but I'm a guy you don't want in your play because I can take you . . . you'd be dead meat."

Danny, a bit surprised at this complete stranger mouthing off, turned to his friends, then sized up David, saying, "Ok wise-ass, come to the theatre tomorrow . . . we'll go a few rounds."

They did. Danny was impressed. David got into *Knockout.*

Anthony Quinn

1. After a walk-on part or two and some bits in B-movies, Quinn felt he'd never get a speaking role. Told he was too dark, too Mexican, too offbeat, he decided to go out to sea as a fisherman, thinking a change was needed. On the docks, he picked up an L.A. paper and saw an ad: Paramount was looking for actors for Cecil B. DeMille's next picture, *The Plainsman*. Actors were needed who could pass for American Indians. Quinn felt it was worth a shot. He thumbed a ride back to Hollywood, walked very boldly into the casting director's office at Paramount and announced, "Mr. DeMille wants to see me."

"What about?"

"I hear he's looking for a young Indian."

"And *you* are the young Indian," he said warily. (He had seen Quinn before and knew he was no Indian).

"Ksai ksakim eledski chumblum."

Casting director: "What's that?"

"Cheyenne. I speak it fluently."

"No kidding? . . . That's Cheyenne?"

"Of course it is, how could I make it up."

The "full-blooded Cheyenne" had his first speaking part.

2. Quinn tells this story:

Before I was officially hired for the part of Auda Abu Tayi (*Lawrence of Arabia*), I had to meet with David Lean (the film's director) for his final approval. It was a formality, but the producers were paying me a lot of money, and I wanted them to think it was well spent.

Lean was already on location, in the middle of the desert shooting the picture, so I went to see him in costume. I stopped at the production headquarters and had Iolanda outfit me in the appropriate robes. Next, I visited the makeup tent, and showed the artists there a picture of Auda

Abu Tayi. An hour later, I emerged with Abu Tayi's beard and famous hooked nose, looking to all the world like the man himself.

I drove with Iolanda in a jeep to a dune a few miles away. We stopped about a thousand feet from a dramatic cliff, on the other side of which I knew I would find Lean, shooting the day's scene. I ditched the jeep where it would not be spotted. I wanted to make a dramatic entrance, appearing out of the sands on foot.

I had not counted on the locals. Up ahead, beneath the overhang of the cliff, sat four or five hundred Arabs, escaping the midday sun. They were huddled together like sheep. They spotted me on the horizon, and began to chant: Abu Tayi, Abu Tayi, Abu Tayi. To them, I was Auda Abu Tayi, come to lead them out of the hot sun, as if from a mirage. They fell in line behind me, and followed me to the other side, where I had been told I would find the crew. As I walked, the Arabs continued with their chant, churning it into a raving song. Their voices lifted me, and carried me straight to the set where Lean was consulting with Peter O'Toole.

I was told that the Arabs made quite a commotion, which I could see, and that I made quite an entrance, which I could not.

Lean looked up from what he was doing and asked one of his assistants about the ruckus.

"It's just the Arabs, sir," the assistant replied, "They're chanting for Abu Tayi."

"And who the hell is that, at the head of the line?" Lean wondered.

"I don't know. It must be Abu Tayi."

"Well," Lean said, "Screw Anthony Quinn. Let's hire that guy instead."

Gregory Hines

Hines tells this story:

I heard that Robert Evans was going to direct *Cotton Club* and that he was interested in me for the Cab Calloway part. I went to my agent and said, "I've got to see the script."

He said, "No, Evans won't let anyone see the script." But the script was actually in his office, so when he was called away, I took the script in the men's room for about an hour, and read it. I could see that Calloway wasn't the part for me.

I wanted the main black part. I asked for a meeting with Robert Evans—the easiest way to get something is to get directly to the guy—and I went with my hair slicked back, wearing a '40s suit, and told him I wanted that part. He said, "But the part of Cab Calloway . . ." I said, "I don't want that part. I won't do it. I want this part."

He said, "I offered it to Richard Pryor, and if he wants it, he's the man. I can get another seven to ten million dollars of financing with his name, with you, I can get maybe fifteen hundred dollars."

I could understand his point, but I said, "You're making a big mistake."

After I left his house, I did as much research as I could on Richard Pryor, and I found that he'd already committed himself to doing *Superman III* and *The Toy*. Once I found that out, I instituted a reign of terror on Robert Evans. I called him every day. I went over to his house twice again, uninvited. It got to the point where he was actually yelling at me over the phone, "Stop calling me! I know you want the part." At first he liked it. Then when I started calling him every day, his people would answer the phone and say, "You can't talk to him."

I would say to them, "Look, I'm going to get this part. And after I get this part, he's going to love me, and I'm going to tell him how rude you were to me. So you get him on the phone and let me talk to him. Because if you don't and I get this part, you're out and I'm in."

Gregory Hines was in *Cotton Club* playing the part he wanted to play.

Warren Beatty

After co-starring with Natalie Wood in the movie *Splendor in the Grass*, Warren set his sights on the co-starring role of the young Italian gigolo opposite Vivien Leigh in Tennessee Williams's *The Roman Spring of Mrs. Stone.* On his way to the airport to get a flight to London, he heard that Vivien and the director, José Quintero, approved of his playing the part, but that Tennessee had final casting approval and was adamant that the part be played by a bona fide Italian.

Undeterred, Warren changed his flight and caught a plane to Puerto Rico, where Tennessee was vacationing. As Warren recalls:

"I walked up to him in a gambling casino and began to talk to him in an Italian accent . . . and I brought him a glass of milk on a tray, because I had heard he had ulcers from his reviews of *Sweet Bird of Youth*.

"He fell on the floor and said, 'All right, all right, you've got the part.'"

Adam Sandler

It has been said that Adam, early on in his career, while auditioning for Lorne Michaels, the executive producer of *Saturday Night Live*, humped a chair and was signed to a five-year deal on the spot.

Danny DeVito

Danny came to Los Angeles from the New York theatre scene saying he wasn't going to do any television, until he got the script for *Taxi*, which he thought was very well written, "pretty good stuff." Television was all new to him and he went in for what he assumed was a cold reading in front of some big TV names, James Brooks, Stan Daniels and some ABC executives. DeVito figured he didn't have a chance. He stood up with the script, looked at it then looked up at the men in the room and said, "Who wrote this shit?"

Everyone in the room lost it, they broke up. They had their Louie DePalma.

Dabney Coleman

Buffalo Bill, an NBC-TV show starring Dabney on the air for one year, had ratings problems. The character that Dabney played was a cantankerous, free-wheeling host of a talk show, and the show's future didn't look too bright.

At a meeting of the department heads and the boss of NBC-TV, Brandon Tartikoff, Dabney appeared dressed as Buffalo Bill. The subject: will Dabney and "Bill" come back in the fall? There was a lot of talk. Dabney listened. The talk ended.

Dabney then jumped up and went nose to nose with Brandon, shouting, "What's it goin' to be? Let's hear it. Is there another season? Say it . . . yes? No? I want to know!!!"

Almost overwhelmed, Brandon, "Yes, yes, all right, you got the show." After, Brandon said, "He deserved it" after that great performance that day.

Camryn Manheim

Frustrated by the absence of roles for larger women, Camryn wrote a one-woman play called *Wake Up, I'm Fat!*, from which her book takes its name. A funny, touching monologue about her life as a fat woman, the show won her the attention of Randy Stone, V.P. of casting at 20th Century Fox. Stone called Camryn to Los Angeles to meet with David E. Kelley, the creator of *Picket Fences* and *Chicago Hope,* who was casting a new TV show about lawyers at a Boston firm: *The Practice.*

Camryn desperately wanted a part, but she recalls that after their brief meeting, Kelley looked so uninterested, she thought he might doze off.

On her way out, she spotted a cribbage board, announced to Kelley that she could "beat the shit out of him." Kelley responded, "I don't think you understand, I play the computer." Camryn said, "I don't think you understand, I play for money."

He didn't take her up on the cribbage challenge for several months (she won), but he did write a part for her.

Jackie Cooper

Jackie's mother had two jobs: days, a secretary; nights, playing the piano for some songwriters working on a musical at Fox Studios. In the musical was a spot for a five- year-old boy singer.

Jackie's mother arranged an audition for him. Why not? She taught him the song at home. Jackie picked it up in no time. Then she had Jackie's grandmother come with him, pretending she was his mother. She also coached Jackie to not recognize her at the audition. She made it into a game they were playing, and Jackie loved games.

Jackie did his song, got the job, and nobody ever caught on to the great acting job the five-year-old boy pulled off.

Mitch Ryan

At the old Circle in the Square Theatre downtown in New York City, Michael Cacoyannis, the internationally known film and stage director, was auditioning actors for his production of *Iphigenia in Aulis* starring Irene Papas. Ryan, auditioning for the part of Agamemnon, had worked hard preparing for the role but felt he needed a little "support." Before the reading he had a few drinks in the bar next door to the theatre.

Ryan read the scene several times with Cacoyannis suggesting line readings here and there. After the audition, Ryan, about to leave, realizing he was flat broke, asked Cacoyannis for twenty dollars. Taken aback by the request, he nevertheless gave him the twenty and asked him when he would get it back.

"The first day of rehearsal," said Ryan.

Later Cacoyannis said he *had* to hire him to get his money back.

Bea Lillie

In 1914, the Toronto-born Bea arrived in London eager to show English audiences what she could do. After many frustrating auditions, Bea heard that the renowned London revue producer André Charlot was seeing talent for his next show. Bea, with her repertoire of offbeat, whimsical songs, felt she was a perfect fit for a revue-type show. She also heard that Charlot was tough taskmaster who knew what he wanted and got it. Armed with that knowledge, Bea got an audition, ready to give him all she had. Ah, but instead of Charlot, Bea was faced with his business manager.

Not to be put off, Bea opened with one of her favorite numbers, "Oh, for the Wings of a Dove." The business manager barely had time to react to it when Bea immediately went into her next song. At the finish, he responded with the cliché "We'll get in touch with you."

Bea pleaded with him to do another, to which he agreed, and then another. By this time he had heard enough. He got up from his chair, but Bea jumped in with "This will be the very last, I promise."

Appealing to his sense of God and Country—mind you, this was wartime—she sang, "God save our gracious king, long live our noble king . . ."

That did it. He hired Bea for the next Charlot Revue.

Margaret Hall

Being seen for the part of Helena in Shakespeare's *Midsummer Night's Dream*, Margaret was turned down because she was too tall.

"Get tall actors," she replied.

Abe Vigoda

What do you get from an eighty-year-old actor who doesn't need to audition anymore? Advice. Abe feels actors do the same monologues over and over that people at auditions are tired of hearing them. When he had to audition, like everybody else, Abe wrote an audition piece for himself, about a carnival barker. He says it was the secret to his ongoing success as an actor.

Lee Wilkof

Wilkof tells this story:

After jumping through various hoops put in my path by Dustin Hoffman's major domo Stanley Beck, I secured an audition for the revival of *Death of a Salesman* in Los Angeles. For the role of Bernard, I was to read for Dustin and Arthur Miller.

I read.

Arthur and Dustin huddled. "We like what you did very much," said Mr. Miller, "but we already have a bald fellow cast in another role."

"I have a toupee," I cried. But as I said it I realized that it was in New York. "That's wonderful, come in tomorrow and show us," said Arthur.

I left the audition elated and panicked. How could I get my toupee by tomorrow? I came up with a plan! My toupee was made in L.A. by a wig-master named Ziggy. I called him and asked if he had any toups I could borrow for the audition. "Come over, we'll find zomzing," he said in his Austrian accent.

Well, long story short, he made all of Burt Reynolds's pieces, and lent me one he had hanging aroud his workshop. It fit and was close to the same style I had.

I went back to Arthur and Dustin, and as I was about to start reading, I said, "By the way, this is Burt Reynolds's hair piece."

Dustin said, "I hope it doesn't rub off on you."

Ron Liebman

Liebman shares this story:

The play was the highly controversial *The Deputy* by Rolf Hochhuth, about secret agreements between the Vatican and the Nazis, and specifically about the Pope and Pacelli, regarding the rounding up and deportation of Italy's Jewish population. The producer Herman Shumlin's office was bombed the night before my audition for the role of Captain Salzer, head of the SS in charge of the roundup. Shumlin had offered me another role but I wanted to play Salzer. Shumlin said he'd *never* give me the role.

So I rented an SS uniform—which turned out to be an actual SS uniform, not a costume—complete with swastika, skull and crossbones, jackboots, riding crop, etc. The day of the audition, I spent over three hours in my cellar apartment in Greenwich Village getting into makeup: cropped hair, nose putty, pale war-weary grease paint, lines and shadows for age, and so on (I was way too young for the part).

As the audition time neared, I went out to discover it had been snowing heavily for hours . . . no traffic, no cabs

. . . it's the subway in full Nazi regalia. The wonderful thing about New York; no one gave me a second glance, "Oh, just another New York lunatic."

I arrived at the theatre and informed the stage manager I'd be hiding in the basement so Shumlin wouldn't see me before the audition. I hid in the shadows. The backstage phone was in the basement. I heard footsteps coming down the stairs; it was the producer/director, Shumlin, his bald head gleaming from the glow of the swinging light bulb above the phone. Shumlin didn't see me and as he made his call, I thought, "It's now or never, Herr Salzer!"

Standing in the shadows behind Shumlin, I lightly struck the swinging light bulb with my riding crop and in my best German, said quietly, "Shumlin, Herr Shumlin? Vas ist das, Juden?"

Shumlin, who suspected neo-Nazis had bombed his office, turned around in horror and screamed! I yelled, "Shumlin, I've got you!" He shrunk back and after a beat said, "Liebman, you bastard!"

I thought, well, I've got the part. He still made me audition! I got the part and played Captain Salzer for nine months at the Brooks Atkinson Theatre.

Roy Scheider

Scheider shares this story:

As a young actor, I had won a couple of acting awards, like the Theresa Helburn Opdyke Award. Theresa Helburn was one of the founders of the Theatre Guild. I was brought to her apartment in New York, where she served these awful martinis.

Then when I was in the Air Force, I used to get letters from her saying things like, "I know it rains a lot up there, be sure and wear your rubbers." Like my mother! I thought, hell, when I go back to New York, I'll walk right into the

Theatre Guild, and I'll be on Broadway in two weeks. Well, she died six months before I came back to New York.

At the time, the Theatre Guild had just had a very successful tour in Europe with Helen Hayes and Mary Martin in *Skin of Our Teeth*, *Glass Menagerie*, and *Miracle Worker*. Now they were planning a tour of South America. Lawrence Langner, Theresa's partner, was holding auditions and try as I might, I could not get an audition. Then one day I stormed into his office and said, "Tell me that if, Theresa Helburn was alive, the two-time winner of the Theresa Helburn Award couldn't get a goddamn job?" I got three: stage manager, understudy, and a small part.

Sean Hayes

An independent gay film Sean appeared in was opening at Robert Redford's prestigious Sundance Film Festival. NBC sent Sean a new sitcom script, *Will and Grace*, hoping to grab his interest. Sean found it a hoot, unlike many other sitcoms, but he passed on it—actually throwing the script away—since it meant he would have to pay to fly back to L.A. to audition. However, NBC kept pushing Sean to try for the part of Jack, Will's good buddy. Finally he went in and did a Jack thing. As he left the audition, he ad-libbed, "Stop looking at my ass, Mutchnick."

Executive producer Jason Mutchnick knew he had his Jack. Sean was later quoted as saying, "When I came out of my mom's womb, I had sitcom stamped on my forehead."

Joe Viterelli

Anyone who saw the De Niro/Crystal comedy *Analyze This* could not forget Joe's face and character. So, naturally, Joe was invited to read the part of Jelly in the sequel, *Analyze That*. After several different read-throughs, Joe realized that he was one of the few actors who kept coming back to read and Joe figured he had the part.

Later he got a call . . . they wanted him to read for another part, not Jelly. But Joe asked to read Jelly again, and then they could decide one way or the other. He read Jelly.

After the reading they thanked Joe for coming in . . . that's it. As they were leaving the building on the sixth floor, Joe stopped them and said, "If I don't get the part of Jelly, I'll throw you out of the fuckin' window."

Joe got the part of Jelly.

Kirk Douglas

Hollywood producer Stanley Kramer's biggest concern in casting his fight picture *Champion* was finding a lead actor who could not only act but be convincing as a professional boxer. "Having interviewed countless unsuitable prospects, I was becoming anxious about this problem when a handsome young actor came into my office one day. He had done a few plays and small parts in films. He looked the part . . . lean, yet muscular. With training by a pro I felt he could do it . . . but could he act?

"Douglas had a look of determination and in talking about the role he seemed to really understand the character . . . with every word he spoke. Finally, in an impassioned plea, he ripped off his shirt to show me his muscles, then shook his fist at me and cried out, 'I can do it! You know I can do it.'

"He convinced me. I hired him without ever seeing him on stage or screen."

Anthony Mackie

Mackie enters a room where he is auditioning for a film. Waiting to read with him in the room is the casting lady. The quiet and still atmosphere of the room is broken by the very assertive entrance of the film's producer, the CEO of rap's Rocafella Records, Damon Dash, accompanied by four assistants. They converge at the table and take their seats flanking Damon, who says to Mackie, "Ok, actor."

As Mackie begins to read, Damon is on his cell phone talking. In a minute or two his assistants are dealing with pagers. There's a whole lot of talking going on while Mackie struggles on until he cannot continue.

"Are you people going to keep this up? What is this?"

"What's your problem, actor?" Damon asks.

"I'm not reading if you all are going on with the phones and beepers."

Damon stares at Mackie with that who-the-hell-is-this-guy look. He looks down at Mackie's resume, then looks up. "You're from Juilliard School, huh? Ok Juilliard actor, let me see you act."

Mackie picks up where he left off when the cell phones and pagers start up again. Mackie stops, takes a deep breath and says, "How do you expect me to act with all this crap going on?"

"How's that? Who the hell do you think you are, Juilliard?"

"Who the hell are you? You're just trading off your cousin Stacey's name. At least she's an actress."

"What? Do you know who the hell . . . ?" Damon, now enraged, gets up, grabs the table, overturns it, sending papers and phones flying. He lunges toward Mackie who stands his ground.

"What are you going to do, hit me? C'mon, I'm not afraid of you."

Before Damon can get to Mackie, his assistants grab him, hold him, and drag the screaming Damon out of the room. Mackie stands there for a moment in the suddenly quiet room and as he turns to leave he hears giggling . . . it's the casting lady, her head bowed, barely able to contain herself.

Joe Morton

Nikos Psacharopoulos, artistic director of Williamstown Theatre Festival, was seeing actors for Kenneth Cavander's adaptation of the *Oedipus* cycle to run for two consecutive evenings. Joe was auditioning for the part of the messenger, but he really wanted to play the title role. However, Nikos had offered it to another actor, and when that actor had to drop out, Joe, one of America's most versatile black actors, insisted on reading for Oedipus.

Nikos had Joe come in and read. A few days later, Nikos saw him again. They talked. Nikos liked what Joe did with the part, but he didn't know Joe, he didn't trust him. They spent the next few days working together . . . learning to trust each other. Then one night Nikos called: the part was his.

But Joe, meanwhile, had a film offer; he would be a week late for rehearsals. Nikos didn't panic, and they worked out the schedule to accommodate each other. They'd learned to trust each other.

Sheldon Leonard

In the thirties, an old friend and Group Theatre member, J. Edward Bromberg, got Sheldon interested in acting. Sheldon had been doing odd jobs, but Bromberg truly felt Sheldon had a talent for theatre and he began to advise him on where to go and what to do.

One day Sheldon got a reading with the Broadway producer Brock Pemberton in his office. Brock liked Sheldon's reading and asked him what he had done professionally. Luckily, Bromberg had prepared Sheldon for that question, saying he should "make up a list of out-of-town jobs nobody's going to check up on you."

Sheldon said, "I had two years with the Jessie Bonstell Repertory Company in Detroit playing heavies and second leads. I was with Cukor Randolf in Rochester for a year, then I did a year and a half with the Chicago company of *Abie's Irish Rose.*"

Smiling, Brock said, "Okay, what's your salary?"

Bromberg hadn't prepared him for that. Sheldon guessed, "Twenty-five dollars a week."

The equity minimum at the time . . . forty dollars a week. The interview ended.

Warren Oates

A character actor, Warren has been seen in many Sam Peckinpah films, including the classic *The Wild Bunch*. He studied in New York, did part-time jobs and a lot of extra work. Dan Petrie was directing the TV show *U.S. Steel Hour*, and there was a part in it right up Warren's alley.

He figured the only way to get into that office was to pull a stunt. So he ran up the stairs to the fifth floor, went into the office and told the secretary that he had a one-hundred-and-fifty-five-pound package for Mr. Petrie.

She said, "What is it?" He told her he didn't know. So she called Mr. Petrie to the door.

"What is this," he asked, "you have a one-hundred-and-fifty-five-pound package for me?"

Warren said, "Yes, it's me!"

It broke Mr. Petrie up . . . Warren didn't get the part.

Peter Hunt

Hunt tells this story:

My favorite audition of all time was Richard B. Schull, who has, as you know, been in a lot of commercials. All he did was come out and somehow he exuded this aura of "You can do anything you want with me. I'm just here and whatever." You just smelled good things when he walked out from the wings. He wears a suit and a funny bow tie and sneakers, and it gets to be bizarre, but it isn't bizarre; that's just it. He always sings "Lost in the Stars" and he can't quite sing it and so you start laughing at him and you think it's a clown act and then about halfway through you realize it isn't. It's more like Walter Houston singing, and it grabs you and you get a lump in your throat and you realize this guy is really serious.

But when he finishes the audition you know he's just kind of a nice guy. It's a wonderful audition. Best one I've ever seen. You have a feeling he wants the job but the audition isn't the first and last audition he's going to do. There's that marvelous balance between "I'd love to be in your play but this isn't the end of the world." So he puts you at ease.

I think that's one of the hardest things; if the actor can put the director and the producer at ease, because they're just as nervous, they have a terrific chance of at least being heard.

William Duell

1. Up one morning, promptly at ten o'clock, Bill was being seen for some commercial. There was no copy. He was told, "Be bacon in a frying pan, lay on the floor." This did not deter Mr. Duell; after all, was he not a Yale Drama School graduate (MFA)? His bacon did not sizzle as much as he had convulsed them. Mr. Duell used a "substitution," he had an epileptic fit. Mr. Duell left muttering, twitchingly, misquoting Shakespeare, "We precious few . . . will not forget St. Crispin's Day."

2. An actor friend of Mr. Duell tells of a commercial he went up for. He forgot the product, but not the audition. He walked into the office and they poured water on him just to see how the water dripped down on him. He got a callback! . . . And they poured water on him again!

No, he didn't get the job . . . but, all-moist!

Estelle Getty

In the latter part of the eighties, the head of NBC's programming, Brandon Tartikoff, decided that the older population wasn't represented enough on TV, which led to the creation of the show *The Golden Girls*, about four older women living together in Miami, Florida. Three of the women had been cast, but Bea Arthur's eighty-year-old mother was yet to be determined. Estelle Getty, in her early sixties, had auditioned twice but was turned down because it was felt "she didn't look old enough to play eighty."

She was able to get a third audition, and this time she was ready. She dressed more for the age and said to the makeup man, "To you this is just a job. To me, it's my entire career down the toilet unless you make me look 80."

The makeup man's job did the trick. Estelle played Bea Arthur's mother for seven years and got two Emmys along the way.

Chapter Four
Nervous?

Will Ferrell

Becoming a member of the illustrious, long-running hit comedy show *Saturday Night Live*, goes like this: First, an initial audition; then, a meeting with the executive producer, Lorne Michaels; and later, a second audition. Will had passed the initial audition and was scheduled to meet with Lorne.

Will had heard that other performers who had succeeded did something outrageously funny, so he decided to come up with a plan he thought could work. He would walk into the meeting with a briefcase filled with fake twenty-dollar bills and during his meeting with Lorne, find the moment to start stacking all the money on Lorne's desk.

Then Will planned to say, "Lorne, we can talk till the cows come home, but we both know what *really* talks is cold, hard cash. Now I'm going to walk out of this room, and you can take this money or not. Do with it what you wish. No one will ever know. And then we'll talk about this little *Saturday Night Live* thing." . . . Leaving Lorne thinking, "Wow, what a ballsy, clever guy! I must hire him immediately!"

Pleased with his plan, Will waited outside Lorne's office, briefcase on his knees. Ushered into the office, Will quickly sensed the atmosphere was all business. Lorne told him what he was looking for, asked about his strengths. They then ran over the audition pieces Will had chosen, Lorne rejecting some of them, all the while staring at the briefcase . . . wondering "a comedian with a leather briefcase?" The meeting ended. Will left with the unopened briefcase.

Two weeks later Lorne asked to see Will again, and this time Will was determined to try the suitcase bit. At Lorne's office, Will was met by the assistant, who said, "Oh, you won't be needing the briefcase, you can leave it with me." Will, too embarrassed to admit it was part of his comic bit, left the briefcase behind.

In the office, Lorne, after a talk with Will for twenty minutes, hired him as part of the *Saturday Night Live* cast. Will, thankful and happy, left and then explained the whole briefcase plan to the assistant. He pulled out a stack of fake twenties and told the assistant to give it to Lorne as a token of his gratitude.

Anthony Hopkins

Feeling terribly anxious because he was auditioning for the prestigious National Theatre (London) and that his audition pieces weren't very good, Tony felt particularly nervous doing a speech from *Othello* since Sir Laurence Olivier was then playing Othello, and brilliantly. But to learn a new piece now was foolish. When Tony walked in the theatre he still couldn't accept the fact he was meeting the great Olivier. In truth there was Olivier sitting there wearing glasses and a three-piece suit saying to Tony, "Hello, how are you, dear boy? What are you going to do for us?" At a table sitting were a few other directors and casting people.

Tony: "A bit of Chekhov, Tusenbach in *The Three Sisters*, and *Major Barbara*."

Olivier: "And for Shakespeare?"

Tony: "*Othello*."

Olivier: "*Othello*? You've got a bloody nerve!"

Tony: "It's the only Shakespeare I know."

He did the first two pieces and to put himself at ease, he put his hands in his pockets. His hand came out to emphasize something and with it a comb and handkerchief. But he somehow finished.

Olivier: "What are you going to do for dear old *Othello*?"

Tony: "The scene in the bed chamber."

Just before Tony began, Olivier asked someone for a cigarette, then turned and said, "I'm terribly sorry, I'm so nervous in case you're better than me," in his charming manner to put Tony at ease. Tony did the scene. Olivier came up to him and said, "Well done. I don't think I'll lose any sleep tonight, but . . . you're awfully good. Would you like to join the company?"

Tony was thrilled to become a member of the Royal Shakespeare Company.

Elaine Stritch

When an aspiring eighteen-year-old actress, Ms. Stritch heard that the Richard Rodgers office was sending out a road company of the musical *Oklahoma*, she sensed a golden opportunity. However, Ms. Stritch had a problem. She had no agent. What to do? You pretend.

Ms. Stritch pretended she was Beatrice Fix, an agent who was submitting a client. The Rodgers office replied they never heard of her. Ms. Stritch said she was an independent agent. It worked.

Her audition was for the character Ado Annie's "I'm Just a Girl Who Cain't Say No." At home, nervous and scared beyond belief, Ms. Stritch bathed, did her hair, changed her clothes three or four times, fastidiously chose the right accessories and shoes with the Dior suit she picked out.

Jittery with anticipation on the Fifty-Seventh Street crosstown bus, she became aware of murmurs around her.

Puzzled, she looked around and following some of the staring faces, she looked down and realized she had forgotten to put on her skirt with the suit. She was wearing her slip!

With great dignity, she managed to "rearrange" herself, got off the bus, went home to get more appropriately dressed, arrived in time for the audition, after which Richard Rodgers remarked, "You're talented, go study."

Jack Black

Like many funny people, he spends an inordinate amount of time worrying about whether he's funny enough. Before he became a star with *School of Rock*, he nearly pulled out of what became his breakthrough film, *High Fidelity*, for fear of embarrassing himself.

The director, Stephen Frears: "Once he realized he'd been offered the part, he panicked and suddenly said he wouldn't do it. I said, 'What do you mean, you won't do it?'"

Jack said, "Well, you didn't make me audition . . . auditioning gives me confidence."

Stephen Sondheim

Jeff Saver, a musical conductor in his own right and an accompanist for many singers at auditions, tells of one session involving one of the giants on the American musical theatre scene, Stephen Sondheim.

After seeing and hearing one singer after another at this one audition, Mr. Sondheim, who loves performers, felt compelled to ask his casting person, Joanna Merlin, seated nearby, "Why are they all so nervous?"

Joanna, a noted actress herself, looked at him in surprise, "Because you're here."

Mr. Sondheim slid down a little in his seat at the realization that his presence, unknowingly, had such an intimidating effect on the singers.

Gene Wilder

Mel Brooks, writer and creator of the movie *The Producers*, had already signed Zero Mostel for one of the leads, Max Bialystock, and when he saw the Broadway play *Luv* he offered the second lead, the accountant, to Gene, whose only prior film work was in the movie *Bonnie and Clyde*. Backstage with the movie's producer, Sidney Glazier, Mel told Gene that Zero didn't know him and that he was sorry to say that Gene would have to read with Zero.

Gene, who had believed that no audition would be necessary, was *intensely* nervous about meeting and reading with Zero. "My heart was pounding as I walked to Sidney Glazier's office . . . and up the elevator my heart was pounding harder. I knock at the door. There's Mel and Sidney and Zero.

"Zero gets up and walks toward me and I'm thinking, 'Oh God, why do I have to go through this again? I hate auditions, I *hate* them.' Zero reached out his hand as if to shake hands and then put it around my waist and pulled me up to him and kissed me on the lips . . . a big kiss on my lips and all my fears dissolved." They read. Later, Gene was called. He was Bloom . . . thanks to Zero.

Alfred Lunt

Jacqueline Bertrand went to see Mr. Lunt, who was directing a play on Broadway. Before the audition she was advised to watch out for his one glass eye and to avoid staring.

"This kind, wonderful man came up on stage to read with me! I kept thinking 'mustn't stare.' I couldn't tell which was real and which was false . . . so, of course, I found myself staring and I became totally discombobulated and was at a loss of words. I burst into tears.

"Mr. Lunt was generous and comforting, drying my tears. Before he sent me home he asked me to write him the recipe for French-Canadian meat pie and he'd send me his own flour, which he did.

"I didn't get the part . . . but I made terrific bread from his recipe!"

David Hasselhoff

David, star of the hit TV series *Baywatch*, recalls once going on an interview for a very important role. It was so important, and he was so nervous about the whole thing, that he wet his pants.

Joan Rivers

The Sunday night *Ed Sullivan Show* was the longest-running TV variety show (1948–71). Sullivan had the pulse of America. He introduced the Beatles and Elvis on his show. Joan first did his show in 1967 because of a mistake. By then, Sullivan was getting confused. What happened was, he had agreed to book Johnny Rivers, a folksinger . . . but announced, "Next week we'll be having Joannie Rivers," so he had to get her on the show . . . but Ed wanted to see her act before the final okay.

Joan went to his apartment in the Delmonico Hotel on Park Avenue. He sat behind a lacquered French desk in his living room on a Louis XVI chair. Joan stood in front of the desk like a child before a teacher and said, "My hairdresser, Mr. Phyllis? We're very close. As a matter of fact, he was one of my bridesmaids."

The most powerful man in TV entertainment sat stone-faced. He never smiled. Not once.

Joan continues the story:

"Feeling that I was drowning in the pool of silence, I pushed on.

"'Somebody broke into Mr. Phyllis's apartment, and they took his roommate. They thought he was a piece of pop art.' I was afraid of seeing Sullivan frown . . . I did the whole act to a French Impressionist painting right above his head. 'Hey, the stewardess was such a tramp . . .' I told the gold frame while Ed's wife, Sylvia, sweetly tiptoed through the room.

"I was right back when I first stepped on stage and bombed. When you're successful, audiences take you on faith; they no longer judge you. Here in Ed Sullivan's living room, the jury was still out. I felt sweaty, felt myself shrinking into my skin, felt my shoulders hunch, my feet go pigeon-toed. You can't run screaming from the room in panic, you force yourself to finish, talking too fast, too loud, not waiting for the punch line, swallowing key words of a joke."

Ed must have had an inner chortle that day, because he let Joan go on his show.

F. Murray Abraham

Murray, like many established actors who never audition, but instead field any number of offers or take meetings, not too surprisingly early on in his career had many tough years as a New York actor. He recalled trying to get his foot in the door at Joe Papp's Shakespeare Theatre downtown on Lafayette Street. With very little luck. Seven years of trying, in fact, and absolutely nothing.

Then, hearing that the part of Hotspur in one of the *Henry*'s was being cast—one of those parts that bravura actors like Olivier had triumphed in—Murray, finally, not only got into the door on Lafayette Street, but got to audition for Hotspur. He read. He could see that they didn't want him. He then begged for any kind of part, spear carrier, anything. He was turned down. He walked out totally ashamed. Disappointed beyond belief, Murray left the

building crushed, and in his own words, became catatonic
. . . he literally could not move, he didn't know where he was
standing. Somehow, a woman who knew him was passing by,
stopped and talked to him and managed to get him safely
home.

And for a long time after, Murray couldn't even walk near
the Shakespeare Festival Theatre on Lafayette Street.

Audra McDonald

Auditioning for the musical revival of *Carousel* in New York
a few years ago, Audra sang up a storm and walked offstage
when she finished.

She so impressed the creative team, they immediately
asked the stage manager to bring her back on stage.

The stage manager came out to tell them that she
couldn't possibly come out.

"Why not?" they asked.

"Because she just fainted."

Ralph Richardson

Itching to grow as an actor, the young Richardson applied
to a number of Shakespeare repertory companies headed
by actor/managers, which there were several of in London.
One in particular was kind enough to give Richardson an
audition. After a performance of *The Merchant of Venice*,
Charles Doran, while taking off his makeup, saw Richardson
in his dressing room, a common practice in those days.

"Sit down, Richard, and tell me what you've been doing."
Richardson obliged. Doran asked to see what Richardson
could do.

"Stand over there," he said, pointing to the near wall
where Doran's costume and his own clothes were hanging.
After asking Richardson what he had done, he wanted to
see what Richardson had to offer. Richardson's choice was

Marc Antony's speech from *Julius Caesar*—"Friends, Romans, countrymen," etc.—with broad gestures and passion. In the middle of his oration, Doran cried out "Stop it, man, stop it!"

Richardson stopped, "I'm sorry, Mr. Doran, wasn't it any good?"

"It's all right, it's all right, but you're trampling on my trousers!"

Despite the accident with the clothes, Richardson's bravura rendering of the speech led Mr. Doran to say, "I'm willing to take you on."

Olympia Dukakis

Olympia shares this story:

I got a call about *Steel Magnolias* and was told to go to the Carlyle Hotel in New York City. I was really nervous and hopeful. I went to the desk and asked for Herb Ross's room. They called the room, and presumably I was announced; the desk clerk gave me the room number. I rang the bell several times and someone yelled, "Come in."

The first thing I saw was Herb Ross on the floor in his underwear and an Asian man leaning over him. I was, of course, stunned, thinking I had stumbled upon an interlude.

"Oh, it's you, Olympia, wait for me in the other room," they said.

Did this mean that they would continue and when they finished, I would have my interview?

Ten minutes later, I was called back in and the Asian man was putting on his jacket and leaving the room. I sat and started talking to Mr. Ross, who said he thought I was Lee Radziwell (who he subsequently married) when I arrived. And that Eizo, the Asian, was a shiatsu expert . . . that's all.

Ironically, Eizo, in the intervening years, became a part of my life.

And I always wear a sweatshirt and pants when I see him.

Terence Stamp

Terence's agent arranged for him to meet with Peter Ustinov, who was trying to cast the title role for the movie *Billy Budd*. The character, Billy, when confronted by intimidation, loses his power of speech.

At the screen test Ustinov said, "I'm going to insult you and you try not to speak." Terence didn't and he got the part, not out of the character choice he made, but he was so overwhelmed by Peter Ustinov's presence, he truly was *unable* to speak.

Judy Blazer

Going up to audition for the musical *Titanic*, Judy, who had a ton of credits which included Broadway, was asked to prepare for two different parts, read seven or eight scenes, sing a couple of songs and one of her own. When she asked several times what they wanted to hear first out of all that material, the director kept saying, "Do whatever you'd like to do."

Judy said, "I'd like to go home."

John Frankenheimer

An actor came in to audition for Mr. Frankenheimer, who at the time was seeing people for a film he was directing, and this actor said, "Don't announce me. Just let me walk into the room and do this speech, ok? I'll walk in and do the speech and then I'll leave, allright?" The casting agent said, "Well, sure, sure. . . ."

So this actor goes out the door, comes in, does his speech, finishes it and goes out the door and waits.

John Frankenheimer, through the door, said, "That's right, just keep going . . . don't come back!"

Tyne Daly

Stuart Howard asked Tyne to come in and read and sing for the role of Rose in the revival of *Gypsy* to be directed by Arthur Laurents. Arthur was convinced of her talent and ability to create a "new Rose," so he did not need to hear her, but the producer, Barry Brown, and the composer, Jule Styne, wanted to hear her sing the songs. She auditioned beautifully. The role was hers, but several months later with a large percentage of the money still lacking, two more producers came on board, Fran and Barry Weissler. The Weisslers wanted Tyne to audition singing and reading, not only for them, but for the money people.

Stuart tells this story:

We all assembled at the Winter Garden Theatre, a good luck charm since it had been the home of the very successful Angela Lansbury revival of the same musical. I walked backstage to a very nervous Tyne, said hello and told her that I was kind of embarrassed that she had to audition all over again. And what did that pro reply? "Aw, don't be silly, Stuart, sometimes an audition is the only time we get to really act!" Of course, the audition went beautifully. Everyone was pleased. The money was raised. Tyne opened on the road and, after touring, came to the St. James Theatre on Broadway, winning every kind of award for acting that exists, including the Tony.

David Schwimmer

David's first big audition was for the TV show *Picket Fences*, and he acted his heart out for the network execs. He walked out of the audition feeling he did absolutely the best he could until he went to the men's room and discovered his fly had been open all the time.

Dustin Hoffman

As a young actor (twenty-two years old), Dustin was sent up to read for a Broadway show. Sitting behind a desk was the casting lady, one of the biggest in New York, who did casting for a lot of major shows. The scene was between two men, the casting lady reading the other part. This sort of unnerved Dustin but nevertheless he read the scene, though quietly. When he finished she said, "Sit over here," indicating an empty chair next to her behind the desk.

"Now let's start over." They did it again. "You have to speak up."

Dustin asked, "Can't you hear me?"

"Yes," she replied, "but I just want you to speak up." Next time Dustin spoke louder and she said, "I want you to speak even louder." Dustin said, "But I'm sitting right next to you . . . I spent all these years in class trying to be honest . . . so I'm sitting right next to you, talking to you. Can't you hear me?"

"Yes, I can hear you but how do I know if you're a trained actor or not?"

Dustin said, "I've been studying for a few years." She came back with, "Well how am I supposed to know if you can reach the back of the house? Now once more."

She read her first line, Dustin the second, only he *screamed* it. (He had no idea he was going to do that.) She practically jumped out of her seat, her face red with an expression like, "Who is this psychopath!?!"

Dustin left. At home his agent called, saying, "The casting lady bawled the hell out of me for sending you in and she made me promise to never ever send you up for anything she is casting in the future."

He never heard from her again . . . but in later years Dustin is sure she heard him . . . or of him!

Hermione Gingold

In casting *A Little Night Music*—the Hugh Wheeler/Stephen Sondheim musical, Hal Prince directing—the feeling was not to look for musical-comedy stars with big voices so much as actors who could sing if they had to. One part, the role of Madame Arnfeldt, was up for grabs, and the distinguished British actress Hermione Gingold wanted the part so badly that she even auditioned for it, something she had not done for years.

Prince thought she would be entirely wrong for the part because she was a comedian and he "wanted the humor to flow from the character." Gingold was so sure she was right that she actually appeared at an audition unannounced. She said, "I went down and sang a song I remembered vaguely . . . and Steve said, 'Now would you sing something else . . . and don't speak it quite so much . . . ' and I said, 'I'm sorry, but I only know one song, I'll sing it again if you like.'" So she did and got the part.

In her forty-year career, she had often performed for royalty but never had been so nervous. "Sondheim and Prince were too much for me."

Ivor Novello

A very prolific composer, Ivor wrote a new musical every two years and they were very popular, running about two years each. The English public adored him. He was one of the handsomest men in England and also one of the nicest.

Every two years, from the beginning of his career, a funny little woman with a funny hat and no talent would audition for him and each time Mr. Novello would kindly say, "Thank you very much." She kept coming for sixteen years till Mr. Novello couldn't stand it anymore.

The next time she came to audition he said she needn't because there would be a part in the show for her and that rehearsals start on Monday.

"Oh, but I can't."

"Why not," asked Ivor.

She replied, "But I only do auditions."

Anonymous

Waiting to audition for a world famous director, one actor became so nervous, so intimidated at the prospect of going in to face him, that he lost control of his bowels.

He quickly repaired to the men's room, cleaned up his act, and managed to return and go in to audition.

Nikos Psacharopoulos

Dan De Raey swears it's true:

An actor comes to audition for Nikos, for thirty-plus years the colorful and passionate executive and artistic director of the Williamstown Summer Theatre Festival (Massachusetts). The actor asks Nikos's assistant, "What sign is Nikos?" She says, "Capricorn."

The actor pauses, takes back his picture and resume, turns and starts to leave. The assistant calls after him, "But he's on the cusp!" The actor stops . . . thinks it over . . . comes back, satisfied.

Bob Heller

For a decade or so, starting from the fifties, it seemed as if every aspiring actor and actress in New York wanted to get into the Actor's Studio: It had a great reputation, it was *the* place to study, and stars came out of and practiced their craft there. To get in wasn't easy; one had to audition not once, but often, three or more times before being accepted.

Bob, a longtime member of the studio, frequently was asked to audition with aspirants who felt, naturally, that Bob would know what they were looking for and how to do it. One lovely actress, rather well known, was working with Bob on her audition piece. This actress at the time was married to a famous film and theatre actor who, from what Bob gathered, did not want her to get into the studio.

The day arrived. Just before Bob and the actress were about to climb the stairs to do the audition, the phone rang. It was for the actress. Bob was close enough to hear . . . it was from her husband.

"I hope you fail, you bitch!" . . . She didn't.

Anonymous

As the stage manager announced her name at this audition attended by a group of producers, this very eager and determined young actress authoritatively took center stage, paused, looked out at the expectant faces and . . . froze . . . nothing. She blanked. Not a sound came out of her . . . she was traumatized . . . she had forgotten everything she was going to do.

Out of some desperate corner of her mind, she blurted out, "You're not ready for me yet," and ran off stage.

The next day, she was deluged with calls from the producers.

Paul Mazursky

Mazursky, while casting the three leads in his movie *Down and Out*, was understandably worried and concerned. Richard Dreyfuss had turned his car upside down in an accident, walking out of it alive. But it was clear he had been high on cocaine at the time. When Dreyfuss met with Mazursky, who asked what part he preferred, Dreyfuss said, "I'd be happy to play the dog, Kerouac."

Nick Nolte had been drinking, came in very nervous, read the whole script with Mazursky in an inaudible voice. Mazursky, delicately, asked about his "health." Nolte said, "Fine. Shall we drink to that?" They had a vodka and juice drink.

Bette Midler came in with reddish purplish hair, coat collar wrapped around her face, almost hiding it. She demurely said, "I decked my last director."

"Don Siegel?"

"Yes, I knocked the little bastard on his ass."

Mazursky said, "Then you're perfect for me . . . just don't hit me." The trio of stars were on their best behavior throughout the entire shoot.

Fred Coffin

Fred Coffin shares this story:

I auditioned for a new series pilot. The more I worked on it, the more apparent it became there was nothing of human value in the script. At the audition I was warmly greeted by the "creative team." Then I handed out mimeographed copies of my complete rewrite of the scene . . . silence. I cheerfully announced, "Just read it with me, you'll see."

We read, they laugh spontaneously in spite of themselves. As I left, a writer said, "Funny stuff."

Last I heard from them.

"I do a lot of Off-Broadway—you know, like this."

Chapter Five

When One Door Opens . . .

Marilyn Monroe

James Bacon, Hollywood reporter and ex-lover of Marilyn, ran into her at MGM where her agent, Johnny Hyde, had set up an audition for the movie *The Asphalt Jungle*, directed by John Huston and produced by Arthur Hornblow.

Bacon took one look at her and was flabbergasted. As everyone knows, Marilyn had the most beautiful breasts in town—and she had stuffed her bra with cotton. Bacon tells the story:

"Marilyn," I asked, "what the hell have you done to yourself? You look grotesque. You look like a filing cabinet with the top drawer pulled out."

I could see I hurt her with my bluntness, so I kissed her on the cheek and apologized. But I argued just the same for her to get rid of the falsies.

"They're looking for a girl with big bazooms. Johnny told me to dress sexy."

I couldn't talk her out of it. She went to the audition, cotton and all. A few days later, I saw Huston up at Bogart's house and mentioned the incident to him.

"Well," he said, "I reached into her sweater and pulled out the falsies and said, "Marilyn, now we'll read for the part."

Marilyn had shone in the part in scenes with Louis Calhern, one of the finest actors of stage and screen. A year or two later, he and I were talking about it . . . Louis said, "Jack Barrymore always used to say, 'Never do a scene with a kid or a dog.' After *Asphalt Jungle*, I amend that to include beautiful tits."

Jay Leno

Struggling Jay, out in Los Angeles, hooked up with an agent, but said agent was shifted to another job. Jay then connected with said agent's subordinate, sending him his 8   10 photo, following up with a meeting where Jay was told that things were slow, but he will work with Jay to get moving with him.

Jay, impressed, asked, "Honestly . . . you'll work for me?"

As he was reassuring Jay with his belief in him, Jay's eyes wandered to the wastebasket. In the trash was a photo, ripped in half . . . of Jay Leno.

Jay's comment was: he had heard that an agent's job was "to lie *for* you, not *to* you."

Jennifer Lopez

"My older sister and I started out in musical theatre," says Jennifer Lopez. "She had a great voice and she had more of a chance of making it than I did. But she couldn't take the rejection. You have to get up there and say, 'You like me?' And if they say, 'No,' it's like, 'Up yours! Next? How about *you*? Do you like me? Or you? Or you?' Eventually somebody will say, 'Yes.'"

Peter Boyle

"A big part of becoming a successful, working actor," explained Boyle, "is getting your chops. Becoming fearless. Becoming a lion tamer. Realizing that if you keep doing it, don't worry if it doesn't work once. The next one might. For instance, by the time John Belushi hit *Saturday Night Live*, he'd been working every night for something like five years. You get your chops at Second City and take that attitude with you to auditions. It applies to commercials, which are really little scenes, just as much as it applies to motion pictures."

When Boyle heard that a movie company would be making a low-budget film about a right-wing World War II veteran, he tried out for a role that echoed a scene he'd done at Second City with J. J. Barry. Asked to read from the script, he suggested that he could improvise faster, then proceeded to lose himself in a character he already knew intimately.

Boyle got the part, and the movie, *Joe*, made him a major star. "And there's no way I would have had the chutzpah in the audition had it not been for my Second City training."

George Grizzard

George, who was recently inducted into the Theatre Hall of Fame, has come a long way. His friend Rosemary Harris once told him, "If you're going to be a serious actor, you can't turn your back on Shakespeare."

So George went off to audition for Tyrone Guthrie in Minneapolis. He did a Robert Frost poem and Guthrie just sat there. Finally he said, "I was looking for something more rhetorical." He then said: "Which means you talk loud and then you talk soft."

George went away and brought back the ghost scene from *Hamlet*. Doug Campbell read the Ghost, and he was wonderful, but George felt he sounded like the Mayor of Boystown.

Guthrie told George: "You're a damn good actor, but you don't know anything about this, do you?"

George agreed, but told him that they were a year away from opening the theatre and that he would work on it every day. A week later, George got the call and ended up playing Hamlet in repertory with *The Miser.*

Fred Astaire

Looking at the screen test of Fred, some genius at RKO Pictures wrote a succinct report: "Can't act. Slightly bald. Can dance a little."

A few years later, he became, with Ginger Rogers, Hollywood's biggest box-office attraction.

Jack Nicholson

After Jack's screen test the director reportedly said, "I don't know what we can use you for, but if we ever do need you, we'll need you real bad."

Bette Davis

Her screen test left studio mogul Samuel Goldwyn ranting, "Who did this to me?"

James Cagney

Cagney, one of the all-time greats in Hollywood film history and an Oscar winner (*Yankee Doodle Dandy*), had to be screen tested for the movie *Ragtime*.

Ava Gardner

Ava recalled after her screen test that the director clapped his hands gleefully and said, "She can't act! She can't talk! She's sensational!"

Brad Davis

Rainer Werner Fassbinder, an openly gay film director, said that in auditioning and casting Brad in the film *Querelle*, Brad's white sailor pants were so tight they revealed what religion he wasn't.

Faye Dunaway

In putting together the film *Bonnie and Clyde,* producer and star Warren Beatty considered many name actresses for the role of Bonnie. Among those who turned it down or were not available were Tuesday Weld, Natalie Wood, Carol Lynley, Jane Fonda, and Sue Lyon. Its director, Arthur Penn, came to Warren with a relative newcomer he believed in, Faye Dunaway, who up to that time had made a few films that hadn't been released yet.

In Warren's Beverly Wilshire penthouse, Faye, with Warren, read the first scene where Bonnie stands in a hotel room wearing no clothes, looking out the window to see Clyde Barrow hot-wiring her mother's car. Instead of objecting to the theft, she sees a chance for a more exciting life and flees with him.

"I played that moment like a house on fire and never looked back," Faye said.

Faye's poor southern background made her ideal for the role of Bonnie, and Warren liked her back-country toughness and her reading, but had reservations about appearing with an unknown.

At one point, Faye overheard Warren and Penn talking about her. Penn said, "Either she does it or I don't do it."

When the film was completed, Warren gave Faye star billing.

Charles Grodin

Grodin, early on in his career before *Beethoven*, *Heartbreak Kid*, and *Midnight Run* with Robert De Niro, etc., had an appointment with one of the biggest casting directors in New York, Joyce Selznick. The waiting room was full of actors, and Grodin was told by the secretary that Ms. Selznick was "running late." Actors were being ushered in to read . . . very slowly. One hour passed, then two, then three . . . finally, everyone had gone but Grodin. He rose to his feet to go in when Ms. Selznick came out of her office, hurried past Grodin to the open door of the elevator and disappeared.

Without any sense of apology, the secretary turned to Grodin: "She's running late to dinner."

Shirley MacLaine

The Pajama Game opened at the St. James Theatre on May 13, 1954, and the critics were unanimous. Walter Kerr called it "bright, brassy, and jubilantly sassy." Brooks Atkinson announced, "The last new musical of the season is the best." The *Journal-American* declared, "This is a whale of an evening in anybody's auditiorium." Carol Haney was singled out as the newcomer bound for stardom. But on the show's second night, Haney injured a ligament while warming up and had to be replaced by her understudy, an unknown chorus dancer named Shirley MacLaine.

(Dancer) Buzz Miller said, "Of course Shirley made mistakes . . . she hardly learned the part from Carol before she had to go on. I don't even think there had been a full rehearsal with Shirley. But she went out there and did it like there was no tomorrow."

MacLaine had arrived at the theatre that night intending to quit the show, discouraged into thinking that she would understudy forever. Recalling her unexpected performance, she said, "Somehow I did it. I remember thinking that the cast knows what I'm doing wrong, but the audience doesn't. The only thing on my mind was that I would drop the hat during 'Steam Heat.' I was thinking about the frigging hat, which is what you do when you're a dancer, and dropped it. I muttered 'shit!', picked it up, and went on."

MacLaine's Hollywood career subsequently took off, thanks to film producers Hal Wallis and Bob Goldstein, who were in the audience that night hoping to see Carol Haney in the part. But Wallis was so impressed by MacLaine that he offered the dazzling red-headed dancer a screen test.

Neil Simon

I (Louis Zorich) was being seen for Neil Simon's movie *Out-of-Towners*, to be directed by Arthur Hiller. Fortunately, I was acquainted with both gentlemen; Arthur directed me in two films, and I was Walter Matthau's understudy in the Broadway original *Odd Couple*.

With the film breakdown in his hands, Arthur suggested me for a key role. He and I turned to Neil for a response . . . nothing. Arthur then mentioned another part that I was right for and added a few complimentary remarks about my talent. He and I looked to Neil for a sign, a word . . . nothing. Arthur sighed, gave a glance at the breakdown and saw yet another part I could conceivably do well in and brought it up. He and I, once more, eyed Neil. A long pause, and silence.

Arthur, somewhat rattled, rose from his chair, "Thank you, Mr. Zorich, for coming in." I got up, greatly relieved that the "ordeal" was over, muttered, "Thank you" to Arthur, mainly for really going out on a limb for me, and I suddenly realized that they were the only two words I spoke during the interview . . . and two more than the screenwriter, Neil Simon.

Spencer Tracy

After graduating from the Academy of Dramatic Arts in New York, Tracy knew he could act, but he didn't know if he could make a living at it. In the Broadway casting offices, his own worst enemy was Spencer Tracy. He was not rude on purpose, but his impatience and brashness did not sit well with the men in charge. A mounting prejudice against Irish actors didn't help.

Tracy paid a call at George M. Cohan's office and was unable to get past the secretary, but he left a picture and resume with her. Very soon afterward she phoned Tracy with an invitation to read a part in the new Cohan production; it seemed that Cohan was already familiar with Tracy's acting, which puzzled him. Cohan had not attended any Academy plays.

When Tracy reported to the Cohan office, George M. glared at him and said, "I don't know you at all."

Cohan had mistaken Spencer for Lee Tracy, also a relative newcomer. Spencer Tracy was not given a reading.

Kenneth Mars

At the time, Mars was probably the most sought-after actor in television commercials. "I was doing a lot of commercials and I'd always wind up going down Broadway. I would see Mel [Brooks] on my rounds, and he would stop me and say, 'I'm writing this great picture and you're in it, and you're going to be fantastic,' and so on. Finally, he sent me a script [for *The Producers*]," Mars recalls. "The part he wanted me to play was the gay director, Roger De Bris, . . . I was playing a sort of gay psychiatrist (in a show called *Best Laid Plans*) and Mel loved that character."

Mars came to the audition, but he announced, "Well, De Bris is a good part, but I'm not playing it. I'm playing the German [playwright]."

"No you're not," Mel said. "Yes I am." "No you're not." "Yes I am." Mars was called in three times to read; at last . . . he was hired. It was Mars's first film role.

Don Knotts

Don needed an agent when the TV show he was in (*Steve Allen*) moved to Los Angeles in the late fifties. A good agent was a must, and through a friend he got hooked up with one of the best, Abby Greschler. Abby took no prisoners. He had a tornado of a personality.

One of the first bastions to hit was the powerful MGM studios. No problem. As Abby's car, with Don in the front seat, approached the studio gates, Abby, instead of slowing down, raced right through, the guard shouting and Abby giving him the finger.

At casting, Abby was told by the secretary that the head was in a meeting. Abby said they'd wait. "It's a two-hour meeting." Abby waited till she left; with Don at his side, he charged into the head of casting's office. Four gentlemen were shocked by Abby, who greeted everyone with "Meet Don Knotts, the funniest guy on the *Steve Allen Show*. . . . keep him in mind." And left.

Laurence Olivier

Greta Garbo, in her heyday one of the biggest stars on the MGM lot, was set to star in *Queen Christina*, and her co-star had not been selected. Screen tests were arranged to find the actor and among them was the one of the biggest names of the English theatre, Laurence Olivier. Mr. Olivier wasn't too well known in films at the time, but was right for the part.

Here is where it gets interesting. Part of the screen test was a love scene between Garbo and Olivier, and according to one account, Garbo rejected Olivier, leading one to believe that in filming the love scene, Olivier was found wanting.

In another account, Olivier, who was the choice of the producer, Walter Wanger, and the director, Rouben Mamoulian, complained he was unable to instill warmth into his scenes with a distant and unresponsive actress.

It was no accident, for while Garbo was no longer in love with John Gilbert, a one-time huge star, she wanted him in the film instead of Olivier.

Fred Gwynne

NBC had a sitcom scheduled called *Punky Brewster*. Fred was determined to get to play the guardian of this six-and-a-half-year-old orphan. It was different than anything he had done before. Better known as the star of the hit series *The Munsters*, among others, Fred went out of his way to change his image by coming in with a stylish white suit and hair redone . . . reinventing himself as it were.

Into the audition room bounced Soleil Moon Frye (Punky) to read with Fred; she jumped up on the sofa next to Fred and said, "Aren't you Herman Munster?"

Fred, after all his efforts to radically change his image, was visibly thrown enough to rattle him and to not give his best shot. George Gaynes got the part Fred wanted so badly.

Henry Fonda

Fonda, a movie star for many years, was one of the few major film stars to regularly return to his theatrical roots in New York in plays like *Mister Roberts, Caine Mutiny Court-Martial*, and the one-man show *Clarence Darrow*. On one trip to New York he decided to see a play he heard so much about, *Who's Afraid of Virginia Woolf?* by Edward Albee. He was so impressed with the play that he went backstage to congratulate the cast and to meet Arthur Hill, who played the male lead, George.

The next day Mr. Fonda called his agent to find out why he wasn't considered for the part of George. The agent replied that he was sent the script but turned it down because he felt Mr. Fonda wasn't right for it.

Mr. Fonda fired his agent on the spot.

Jane Powell

Jerry Adler, stage manager for the original *My Fair Lady*, was running the auditions for the lead, Eliza Doolittle, for the national company.

An agent comes on stage with his client, a young girl, and he introduces her: Jane Powell. Mr. Adler takes one look at her and says, "I'm so sorry, but she's too young for the part."

The agent says, "Have you seen her lately?"

John Cassavetes

A door opened for the out-of-work John: a Broadway play, *Darkness at Noon*. He was to replace an actor who was leaving. He read for the producers. They thought he was very right for the part and asked him to see the show. John did. He was then asked if he could reproduce that performance.

"Why would I want to do that?" John said.

"Why would we give you the role?" the producer said, showing him the door.

Patti LuPone

In her own words about not having done the screen test for *Evita*:

"I would not. I couldn't believe that after two years on Broadway, and with the commercial running . . . they wanted me to screen test. I was like, 'You want to know what I look like on camera? Roll the commercial.' And they thought that was an insult. You know what? They insulted me. I don't really care. I would have screen tested and not gotten the role. The only thing an actor has left is his integrity, you know?"

Louis Zorich

Auditioning for a commercial at one of the biggest ad agencies in New York, I'm going over the copy and realizing that it was pretty awful and I am thinking . . . what can I possibly do with this material?

Luckily for me, when I walked into the room to read, the director says to me, "Louis, I really need your help."

A bit puzzled, I ask, "Help? What do you mean? How?"

"Well, the copy is a little lame. Can you make it . . . funny?"

"Funny? What kind of funny?"

"Well, you know . . . funny . . . ah, like, ah . . . the Marx Brothers!"

"You want one . . . or all four?"

Stanley Kramer

Producer of such films as *High Noon, Champion, Ship of Fools, Judgment at Nuremberg,* and *Death of a Salesman,* Kramer said he came to make quick decisions because his method of casting was so different than most Hollywood producers. He seldom relied on screen tests. His method was simply to find someone who made him feel he or she was right for the part.

Alberta Watson

Auditions are not usually fun and very rarely easy, but at some point in your career, you stop trying to second-guess the people who will be on the other side of the table. You pretty much decide what you want to do, you prepare well, and you do it. Alberta Watson tells this story:

"The character in the film I was auditioning for was a New Yorker. I had lived in New York for many years. I was appropriately dressed, clear about my choices, everything was ready. And . . . of course, I was nervous. (I don't care who you are, you're nervous.) Usually there are anywhere from two to six people behind the table but on this day, there must have been twelve people on the other side of the tables. The director, maybe five producers, casting director and miscellaneous assistants . . . *everybody* was there. We did the 'hellos' all around, all very polite. Then they asked me to stand in the hot spot ten or fifteen feet away. The lights and the camera lens were directed at me, which means they could see me but I couldn't see them. It feels very much like an interrogation scene in an old war film. It's unnerving but you more or less get used to it. Just as I was about to start, the director put up his hand to stop me.

"'I know you probably don't like this . . .'

"'Yes.'

"'But I want to give you a direction. I want you to be as New York as you can be.'

"Now . . . I was married to an Italian-American New Yorker and was pretty familiar with the rhythm, attitude, and speech patterns. I knew what to do with her. I don't mind getting direction after they have seen what I have brought to the audition, but to give direction before I have begun effectively negates my work and undermines my preparation. It assumes that I don't know what I'm doing. To me, it was insulting. I resented it. I was silent for a minute . . . and then I said, 'Fuck you' . . . which of course, was what any good New Yorker worth her salt would have said in that situation.

"There was more silence for what must have been ten seconds but felt like an hour. Then the director just smiled. He loved it. A few days later, he offered me the job. But it happened that I was in the lovely position where I could turn him down because I had, in the interim, been offered a better job."

Judith Light

Drama school graduate, repertory theatre for four or five years, then nothing. Broke, on unemployment and nothing in sight, Judith wasn't sure she wanted to stay in the business . . . or try another career.

She decided to quit. Outside, she stared up at the sky and, more to herself, said, "What am I supposed to do? How am I supposed to serve?" It was a moment of pure surrender. She had never been to a therapist before, but felt she needed one for guidance.

The therapist told her not to do anything like quitting acting yet; he felt something was going to happen for her. Later, her agent called; an understudy part on *One Life to Live* was open. That was odd because her agent knew Judith swore never to do a soap opera . . . and to *understudy!*

Wait! She had asked . . . how to serve? Maybe this was it. She went. And found out they were going to replace the actress she was understudying. She was there . . . she read and got the part.

She played it for five years, winning several Emmys, and then starred on *Who's the Boss?* with Tony Danza for eight seasons.

Clark Gable

Clark was screen tested at Warner Brothers in Hollywood by director Mervyn Leroy, and Clark overheard Jack Warner yell at Mr. Leroy, "Why do you throw away five hundred dollars of our money on a test for that big ape? Didn't you see those big ears when you talked to him? And those big feet and hands, not to mention that ugly face of his?"

Within a year the *Hollywood Reporter* announced to its readers that a new star was born.

Polly Bergen

While in Hollywood, Polly caught the eye of producer Hal B. Wallis, who signed her up. He confined her singing to three Martin and Lewis movies and loaned her out to MGM nonmusical endeavors. She disliked watching herself on the screen and left to go to New York to sing and study acting with Lee Strasberg.

But the one MGM musical she did audition for—the Ruth Etting story, *Love Me or Leave Me*—opened a new door. Mervyn Leroy, who was to direct the film, told Bergen her looks and styling were more like Helen Morgan's. That set Polly off. She began incorporating Morgan numbers in her nightclub act.

Morgan's mother was so impressed, she sold the TV rights to her daughter's life to Polly. However, Warner Brothers, which had the film rights for Ann Blyth, wouldn't even audition Polly and tried to block the use of the Morgan songs in the TV version, but the embargo was lifted 105 minutes before the live *Playhouse 90* telecast of *The Helen Morgan Story*, and Polly gave an Emmy-winning performance. Blyth's film was a flop.

Anonymous

Being seen for a part in a play, this actor was asked, "What have you done?"

"About what?"

Tyrone Power

A scout from 20th Century Fox saw Tyrone on the New York stage in Katharine Cornell's *St. Joan* and felt very strongly that Tyrone was right to play the leading love interest to Alice Faye in the musical *Sing, Baby, Sing*. He was tested in New York.

Darryl Zanuck, head of the studio, and his aide, William Goetz, looked at the test in shock and said, "He looks like a monkey!"

Tyrone's eyebrows were quite thick and they seemed to spread across his nose in a straight line. Goetz placated Zanuck: "No problem, we can do something about those eyebrows." Also, the lighting for the test made Tyrone look like a villain.

Retested and with a tweezer job and better lighting and with Goetz's intercession, Tyrone developed into a movie star.

Jackson Beck

Remember the great market crash of '29? Beck did, and how. Employed as a messenger on Wall Street at the time, after not getting anywhere as an actor, Beck was on one of his rounds when he witnessed what would become a common phenomenon. A man apparently fell—or, more probably, jumped—from an upper floor of a building in the Wall Street area and landed right in front of Beck. It was so nerve shattering to Beck that he quit his job. He decided to go back to acting again and see if he could make it his life's work.

He began to hunt for jobs. Blessed with a mellifluous voice, he concentrated on radio, which was very hot in those days; there was no TV. Every network had daytime radio serials, and actors would run from one to another daily, appearing on several different shows. Beck made a plan to visit all the various network offices, ad agencies, and producer's offices. He drew up and followed a map of the midtown area where most of the offices were—block by block, office by office, keeping records of every meeting, every visit, every audition. His plan paid off. He got an agent and never stopped using that golden voice. He worked on hundreds of radio programs, and he was the voice introducing *Superman*, immortalizing the words "It's a bird, it's a plane, it's Superman!"

How ironic. From the man who fell at his feet to the man flying through the air. Quite a jump.

Hobie Nelson

Lynn Lentz tells this story about Hobie:

Hobie was a rare find in the theatre business. He was a kind and thoughtful theatrical agent who began servicing clients for the then General Artists Corporation in the mid-sixties. When faced with the demand for an audition for a new musical by a client, a singer-actress who had triumphed as a star in Broadway's first production of *Kiss Me Kate*, Hobie just couldn't bring himself to tell her that the producers were simply not interested in her at all.

Torn, not quite knowing how to handle it, Hobie thought it over . . . then made the call. He would pick her up in a cab and get her to the audition.

With guilt and no small amount of apprehension, he arrived with her at the stage door, entered the theatre, pushed the actress on stage, handed the pianist her music and said, "Gentlemen, Patricia Morrison!!"

As she finished he grabbed her arm and led her out of the theatre into the waiting cab and drove off without ever revealing his plot to her.

Barry Primus

Barry went to see Jerome Robbins who was directing the play *Oh, Dad, Poor Dad.* . . . After the reading Robbins said, "That's the worst audition I ever heard. Either you're a very talented actor or just an imbecile . . . but since my friend Anna Sokolow [a famous choreographer] recommended you to me, I'm going to give you a small part in the play, and try to find out."

Barry went on to a better part in the play, and later became Robbins's assistant at the American Laboratory Theatre.

Joey Sorge

Joey tells this one:

An older character actor showed up for his audition. He was on time. He waited . . . one hour, then two. Finally, after what seemed like an eternity, he was called in. In the room were the obligatory four or five people to see him.

"For my audition," the actor said, "I'll need your help." This request seemed a bit unusual; nevertheless, someone said, "Okay, what can we do?"

"I'm going out of the room . . . then I'll knock, when I do . . . you just say, 'Who is it?' Ok?" They nodded. The actor then left the room. They sat there waiting . . . waiting . . . waiting. . . .

William Youmans

Bill shares this story:

Years ago, I auditioned for the national company of Sondheim's *Sweeney Todd*. After I sang something from *Brigadoon*, the musical director Paul Gemignani bounced up on stage and said, "You know Bill, you're perfect for this, but your voice is not quite strong enough for this material. Here's my home phone number. Call me on Saturday morning and I'll give you the name of a voice teacher who will develop your voice." I said, "Fine."

Saturday morning I call his number, saying, "Hi, I'm Bill Youmans, I met you at the *Sweeney Todd* auditions . . . you gave me your number to call."

Gemignani: "What? Who is this?"

Bill: "Bill, Bill Youmans from *Sweeney Todd*."

Gemignani: "What? Why are you calling me at home? Never call me at home. Never call me at home. Goodbye."

Cut to ten years later. I'm singing at my third callback of Sondheim's *Assassins* and there's Gemignani again. "Bill, you're perfect for this part . . . the only problem is . . . your

voice is too strong and powerful, Sondheim doesn't like big
trained voices."

James T. Cavanaugh

James tells this story:

In the fall of 1958, my first job in theatre in New York
was an Assistant Stage Manager on a Broadway musical, *First
Impressions*, to be directed by Abe Burrows, produced by
Edward Specter and George Gilbert. My job was to check in
the talent as they arrived at their appointed times.

One day, a nervous, sad-looking woman came in and
asked to speak to George Gilbert. I asked her name, she told
me, hesitatingly, adding: "I'm sure he'll see me." I'd been
instructed not to admit anyone who wasn't on the list, but
she was appealing, and very earnest, and I certainly knew her
name. I told George she was here. I couldn't believe she was
who she purported to be, the pert and perky soubrette in a
Broadway hit from thirteen years before. George rushed into
the anteroom, hugged her, fussed over her, and took her
back into his office. They reappeared a few minutes later,
and she was transformed, now smiling and self-assured. He
stood looking after her as she left.

"What a damned shame," he said, obviously very moved.

"Where's she been?" I asked. "I haven't heard anything
about her for a long time."

"Nobody has. They made her a star during the run of
the show, but she had been trained for operetta, and in the
new, more reality-based musical, there weren't roles for her
anymore, and now that she's a star she couldn't go back to
small parts." Theatre had passed her by.

Lily Tomlin

Lily's first big break came in 1966 when she auditioned for
the TV program *The Garry Moore Show*. Garry loved what Lily

did, but didn't really know how Lily and the characters she played would fit in his variety-based show. At that point, Lily offered to do a tap dance. She took off her shoes and started to tap dance in her bare feet.

Lily had taped the metal taps to the soles of her feet!

That did it for Moore. How could he not have her on his show?

Anonymous

Leaving his trailer, passing by the production offices, this actor, a regular on one of the more popular sitcoms, meets a friend auditioning for a role on an upcoming episode. The friend, a very familiar face from past sitcom successes, excitedly says, "I'm going to get this part, I just know it!"

Curious at his cocksuredness, the series regular asks him why he's so confident. The friend shows him the three-page scene, "There, there, you see?"

Regular: "See what?"

Friend: "The 'yes' . . . the word, 'yes.'"

Regular: "One word? 'Yes'?"

Friend: "Yes! It's all in that one word. I know what to do with it! . . . I just know!"

The next day, the series regular met the casting person.

Regular: "My friend, reading for the part of Berger, got it?"

Casting person: "No, he was too arrogant."

Regular: "Too arrogant?"

Casting person: "Yes."

Juliet Taylor

A long-time casting lady from New York, Juliet says one of the most dramatic stories was years ago when she was casting *Streamers* for Mike Nichols:

Instead of reading with the actors myself, we used young actors as readers who we were a little bit less convinced could actually go on to play the role. And it was an opportunity for them to get Mike Nichols to know them. I saw an actor in a play at the Manhattan Theatre Club and asked him if he would come and be a reader for the day, and it was Peter Evans. By the end of the day, he had the part.

Robin Gammell

Robin Gammell tells this story:

I was invited to read for a part on *Murder One* some time ago. I had worked for Steven Bochco on *Hill Street Blues* so we knew each other. In the Bochco building, a very nice building at Fox, I was sitting in an atrium going over my lines when in walked Steven Bochco. I looked up and did a double take.

"Steven, I thought only mortals came through the front door." He stopped for a moment, took in what I had said in all innocent, pleasant intentions, said, "Fuck you!" and walked on.

I thought I'd pretty much blown the job at that point.

I heard later that Steven had walked into the room where they were auditioning and said, "Robin Gammell's out there. Hire him. Don't audition him, just hire him."

They did audition me, nevertheless, but they also hired me.

Denis O'Hare

Denis shares this story:

Back in Chicago, when I was still temping, I only had one hour for lunch. Trying to squeeze in an audition in one hour was almost impossible. At this particular audition—which was for Rice Krispies, I think—I had been waiting for forty-five minutes. I had to call my temp job and beg them to understand. I waited another half hour. The audition material was dense—a monologue about subliminal advertising where we actually had to say "subliminal advertising" in the audition. Oh, and it was supposed to be funny. Oh, and they really wanted John Cleese but couldn't get him, so we were supposed to channel John Cleese without being English or imitating him. So, after all the wait time, in a black mood and stressed beyond belief, I was finally called in.

I said hello to the seven people sitting behind the conference table. No one said "hi" back. I put on the lapel mike, and the camera operator said in a voice tinged with irritation, "Step back behind the white tape line."

Three sentences in, they stopped me because I said "subliminal seduction" instead of "subliminal advertising." I joked, "Well, that's what it really is." No one smiled back. Start again please.

I started again and made the same mistake. Start again please. I finally got through the whole thing. No laughs. No smiles. Finally, one bored producer said, "You know, you're over thirty."

I pulled the hair on my forehead and said, "Oh, really? You can tell? Is it my receding hairline?"

The producer barked back at me, "Seconds! You're over thirty seconds! It's a thirty-second spot!"

And then I lost it. I said, "You know what, you can keep your *#@*ing job! You *&#ing people have kept me waiting for over an hour! You have no soul. *$# you all!" and I attempted to storm out of the room.

Sadly, I was still attached to the camera with the lapel mike. The mike yanked me back, the camera teetered, and the seven parasitic producers just stared. I tore the mike off and made my parting shot, "You miserable *#@s—I hope this is equal to all your immense talents!" And once again

I stormed out, but part of the mike was still stuck to my lapel and I couldn't get it off my suit.

Shaking with rage, I managed to get out of the door. The casting director just stared at me and said, "What the hell is wrong with you?"

She never called me in again. I never got a commercial. I moved from Chicago to New York and started acting.

"Résumés over there."

Chapter Six
There's No Business . . .

James Dean

Holding auditions for the Jane Bowles play *In a Summer House* a number of years ago in New York, John Styx, the director, sat in the fourth row of the theatre as actors came and went.

One important role, the part of a young man, among others, hadn't been cast yet. No one seemed right until this one particular actor made John suddenly sit up. He was mesmerizing. He was it. John couldn't believe his luck, but from the back of the theatre, sitting and watching, was one of the producers, Oliver Smith.

"No, no, no, not one of those damned method actors!"

The actor who was turned down was James Dean.

Jerry Orbach

Before he was firmly established as the name in the long-running TV hit series *Law and Order*, Jerry, then a relatively unknown actor, faced the usual obstacles of the business. Jerry tells this story:

"They had this insidious computer system called the O-rating, which, when they punch in your name, gives a rating of how many people in this country know who you are. For instance, Lucille Ball would get a 100 on it, and I'll get maybe a 20. Angela Lansbury, prior to doing *Murder, She Wrote*, would have gotten a 20. Now she'll get 95.

"There was one time when I auditioned for a television movie. The director liked me, wanted me. The producer wanted me. I was perfect for the part. Then the network punched up my name on the computer and said, "No, get somebody else who has a more visible name in television.""

Olympia Dukakis

1. From the sublime to the ridiculous. Olympia was sent up to audition for the understudy to three widely different characters in the play *The Aspern Papers*: the leading part, around forty years old (Wendy Hiller); the sixty-ish maid (Augusta Merighni); and, would you believe it, a one-hundred-and-twenty-year-old woman (Francoise Rosay). She would cover all three parts. After a truly inspired reading, the internationally known actor-director Michael Redgrave came running down the aisle of the theatre with great excitement: "Wherever did you come from?"

2. In the middle of Olympia's auditioning for a part in Arthur Kopit's play *Oh Dad, Poor Dad . . .* , the equally famous Jerome Robbins, the director, came running down the aisle of the theatre, saying with great exasperation, "No, no, no, no, what are you doing? It's all wrong, it's all wrong!"

3. Cheryl Crawford, one of the founders of the Group Theatre in the thirties, later became a noted producer. Olympia managed to get to read for one of the key parts in a play Ms. Crawford was producing. The day after the audition, she personally called Olympia to tell her she absolutely gave the best audition, but much to her regret, she could not cast her in the part because the playwright insisted that the part go to his mistress.

Jessica Lange

In the mid seventies, the flamboyant Italian movie producer Dino De Laurentiis announced he was going to do a remake of the 1933 cult classic *King Kong* and that he was looking for a fresh face to play the young girl part (originally played by Fay Wray). Dino was hoping to generate a lot of publicity by his search. Despite auditioning many girls, the right unknown didn't show up.

Getting panicky and frustrated, Dino put out a call to New York modeling agencies. Then a struggling young actress signed with the Wilhelmina modeling agency, Jessica was picked out to test in Hollywood. At the Beverly Wilshire Hotel for four days she worked on the script, then went to Paramount Studios to meet with Dino De Laurentiis.

Seeing her, Dino wanted to send her back to New York. He did not want her. "The first time I looked at her, I said to myself . . . terrible! Here is a girl with nothing at all . . . she isn't pretty enough . . . she has braces on her teeth!" He screamed at Wilhelmina over the phone, for "sending skinny, colorless models."

A few days later, Jessica screen-tested with six other models, moving on and off a temporary jungle stage. Jessica was convinced nothing would come of it. She didn't take it all that seriously. "I didn't have any fantasies."

Jessica was poised to do a scene in bed with a pillow tied to a post meant to represent the ape, King Kong, but without the director present and only the second unit director and a crew looking on very bored . . . when they broke for lunch! But she sat alone on the set till they returned with the director.

They did a scene many times, then another, and the director really began working with her. Mightily impressed, he asked Dino to come to the set and said, "This girl in front of a camera is so fantastic. Dino, you were wrong."

Later he barged into her dressing room and barked, "You have to put on weight! You have to lighten your hair! And take off the braces! Think about getting your nose fixed!"

Max Weinberg

Max and his wife were walking down Seventh Avenue and on the corner at Fifty-Fourth Street, and standing there waiting for the light to change was Conan O'Brien. It was kismet. Max's wife said, "Go over and say hello."

He had just gotten the gig and they had seen him the night before on Tom Snyder's old CNBC show. Nobody knew who he was. Max walked up to Conan and introduced himself from the E Street Band, which sort of put Max in context, but Conan wasn't one of the band's fans.

Nevertheless, Max asked Conan what he was going to do for music for his show. Conan replied, "We have some ideas. Do you have any ideas?" Max said, "I have a million ideas. I'd love to tell you about them sometime."

Conan liked what he heard. Max put together a band in three days, auditioned for the show and got the job as musical director.

Al Pacino

Al first became hot in a play about young hoods, *The Indian Wants the Bronx*, which won him a 1968 Off-Broadway award and a manager, Martin Bregman. His stage roles got him an audition for *The Panic in Needle Park*, a film about down-and-out junkies in Manhattan. "We read a lot of people for the lead role," said Dominick Dunne, the writer who was then a film producer on *Panic*. "It came down to two unknowns: Al Pacino and Robert De Niro. De Niro knelt on the ground, he was actually on his knees, begging me not to give it to Pacino."

The film's distributor, 20th Century Fox, didn't want Pacino to get the role either. "Too ethnic" was the verdict, Dunne said, but the studio relented.

The next studio Pacino would deal with, Paramount, was equally unimpressed. "Coppola tested all four times for the *Godfather*, and Paramount kept saying no," recalls the director of *Needle Park*, Jerry Schatzberg. "And then we sent them twenty minutes of footage from *Needle Park* and Al got the part."

Cole Porter

Frank Milton, who had spent some time in Europe, came back to New York to pursue work in the theatre. Cole's musical *Out of this World* was seeing people, and Frank had the nerve to audition one of Cole's classics, "Just One of Those Things," for Cole himself.

When Frank finished the number, Cole walked down the aisle, with his tiny tie, malacca cane, and boutonniere, and said, "Where did you get your shoes?" Frank said Italy, and Cole said that they were the nicest pair of shoes he had ever seen.

"You must be in the show," Cole said. And Frank was.

Roma Downey

Early in her career, Irish-born Roma thought she was a natural for an Irish Spring soap commercial. "I was up against red-haired girls from all over the United States. I was thinking I was a definite shoo-in because I was the real McCoy," said the star of the hit TV series *Touched by an Angel*.

"They told me that I didn't sound Irish enough."

Charlie Chaplin

David Niven, in his book *Bring on the Empty Horses*, writes the following:

I recounted to Chaplin some of the experiences I had endured in the "meat market," the loathsome practice of some directors, when casting the smaller parts of their films, calling twenty or thirty "possibilities" to the sound stage and making each in turn play a key scene in *front* of the remainder, finally dismissing all except one.

Chaplin told me that this embarrassing and unfair system was a legacy from Broadway and that it had not changed since he had come to New York in 1913 . . . Chaplin was interviewed by William Gillette, a great actor-manager of that time, who was casting for *King Henry V*, and twelve nervous young actors were lined up on the stage, hoping for the microscopic part of Williams, one of the English soldiers.

Gillette, an intimidating figure draped in a long black coat with a fur collar, addressed the group.

"Gentlemen," he intoned, giving full range to his famous voice, "I shall approach each of you in turn and say, 'The dauphin is dead!' Your reply will be one word: 'Dead!' He who makes the most of that one word will play the part of Williams."

The group of young hopefuls shuffled nervously about. At the farthest end of the line in a black suit with a high white stiff collar stood Chaplin, by several inches the shortest. "The dauphin is dead!" boomed Gillette at the first actor, but the young man was so terrified he just managed to roll his eyes and emit a pitiful squeak: "Dead?"

He was dismissed. "The dauphin is dead!" roared Gillette, but the next actor decided that an English soldier would be delighted at the news. "Dead?" He asked, smiling happily as though his stock in the Union Pacific Railroad had risen twenty points. He too was dismissed. As the line thinned out and as an impatient Gillette drew nearer, Chaplin became increasingly nervous. Eight actors had been dismissed with ignominy, taking with them every inflection and every nuance with which he had hoped to embellish the word "dead." Three more dismissals followed in quick succession, and the diminutive Chaplin found himself alone on stage confronted by the towering figure of the now-exasperated actor-manager.

Gillette looked down with distaste upon the sole survivor. "The dauphin is dead!" he yelled.

Chaplin's mind went blank. He shook his head mournfully from side to side, and then clicked his tongue loudly on the roof of his mouth. "Tch! Tch! Tch! Tch!" he went.

Gillette slowly raised his arm, pointed scornfully to the exit, and Chaplin, not for the last time, disappeared alone and with dignity into the sunset.

James Woods

James Woods tells this story:

I worked my way up the ranks. I met a lot of resistance along the way; they always found a reason why they didn't want me. I wasn't conventionally good-looking or I was offbeat. The easiest thing in the world is for people out there to say no. To this day! They didn't want me for *The Onion Field*, I wasn't right for the part. I had to pay for my own screen test. They didn't want me for *Once Upon a Time in America*, I wasn't right for the part. Every movie I've gone up for, I wasn't right for. Finally, I did *Joshua Then and Now* because the director, Ted Kotcheff, said, "You're perfect for this," and Mordecai Richler, who wrote it, said, "You are the perfect one." He's described as a thin, hawk-faced man who's rough and at the same time very bright. Right? So I did it and Janet Maslin in the *New York Times* writes, "Although Mr. Woods is extraordinarily miscast . . ."

Toni Collette

Rob Marshall, director of the Oscar-winning film musical *Chicago*, had some problems casting the leads. Catherine Zeta-Jones had some musical comedy experience and was an easy choice. For the leading lady, Roxie, Marshall auditioned more than a dozen major actresses before deciding on Renée Zellweger, who had little if any musical comedy background. But one actress, Toni Collette (*Sixth Sense, Muriel's Wedding, About a Boy*, Oscar nominee) gave such a stunning audition that she quickly shot to the top of Marshall's list. But no one could be cast without the approval of all "major parties." Ms. Collette was thought to be "too obscure" to carry a film.

Mark Ruffalo

In an interview with Cathy Horyn in *The New York Times Magazine*, Mark talks about the vagaries of Hollywood casting. He figured that before he got the part of Terry in *You Can Count on Me*, opposite Laura Linney, he went on eight hundred film and TV auditions.

"In Hollywood, none of those people can make a decision. They can only say no . . . Casting directors would say, "You are the best actor of your generation, but—you just haven't grown into your face yet, your face hasn't grown into your soul.'"

Phil Silvers

Phil was a big hit in the Broadway musical *Yokel Boy*, playing a brash Hollywood press agent, a Bilko-like character who was the template, Phil later said, for the aggressive, smiling, fast-talking manipulator he would play for the rest of his life.

Louis B. Mayer saw the show and invited Phil out to Hollywood, where the MGM casting department ordered a screen test for him, but preposterously asked him to read for the straight role of an English vicar in the 1940 version of *Pride and Prejudice.*

Silvers's Brooklyn accent made the scene unintentionally funny, but the director said, "This guy can't act." They didn't know he was a funny man. They saw he wore glasses . . . so they treated him like some prime minister or something.

Phil believed that the test, which he later pulled strings to have destroyed, derailed his early film career.

Joan Collins

The Italian film director Renato Castellani was about to do a movie on *Romeo and Juliet,* and the Rank Organization in London decided that their eighteen-year-old contract player Joan Collins would be the perfect Juliet. This did not please either Castellani, since he saw Juliet as a fourteen-year-old virgin, or Joan. The rank organization insisted Joan should be tested, and she was, three times.

Before her final test, Castellani said to Joan, "you will havva the nose job. Giulietta has the Roman nose . . . your nose is not aristocratic . . . go to good plastic surgeon, he make a good roman nose . . . and you be Giulietta."

Joan laughed. "No way, I like my nose . . . in fact one of the newspapers said the three prettiest noses in England belonged to Vivien Leigh, Jean Simmons, and Joan Collins."

After some hysterics and the Italian screaming and yelling, the rank organization backed down and signed an unknown actress who, along with Laurence Harvey (Romeo), was criticized for being miscast. No mention was made of her nose.

Jack Lemmon

Jack won an Oscar for playing Ensign Pulver in the movie *Mister Roberts.* Josh Logan, co-director of the movie with John Ford, directed the play *Mister Roberts* on Broadway. During the filming, Josh asked Jack, "When I was casting the play in New York, where were you?"

Jack said, "I was outside the theatre trying to get in to see you."

Dane Clark

After being considered for the part of a lawyer, Dane, a veteran movie actor, was turned down. Not to be put off, he informed the producer that before he became an actor, he had actually been a lawyer.

"Where was this?" The producer asked.

"New York City," Dane repled.

"Sorry, this is a New Jersey lawyer."

Phil Bruns

Phil is seeing this casting lady for a movie. To get to know him a little, she asks him what he had done. Well, Phil, who goes way back to the Golden Age of live TV in New York, lists *Kraft Theatre*, *Studio One*, *The Jackie Gleason Show*, and *Armstrong-Circle Theatre*, among others. Then Phil starts with his Hollywood credits: film, TV, most of the hit sitcoms—just tons of shows.

The casting lady listens, and then says, "My God, you've worked so much, you really don't need this job, but thank you for coming in, goodbye."

Neva Small

Neva went up to audition for a musical comedy with her own pianist . . . her pianist ended up getting the job.

Grace Zabrieski

Grace, a widely respected actress working in Hollywood, was up for a part she felt she was dead right for but did not get. Disappointed, she called her agent to find out why. The agent told her that the producer, when her name came up, said "Grace, Grace Zabrieski? Oh, she's a real actress, isn't she?"

Anna Kashfi Brando

Anna, working in London at the time, heard that Paramount was doing a picture in France and was searching for an Indian girl. Many girls were seen, and none of them were quite right for the star, who had casting approval and was very difficult. The part needed to speak Hindi, no English.

Anna was born in Calcutta, India. An audition was set up in a Paris hotel where she met Edward Dmytryk, the director of the film *The Mountain*. The story dealt with a plane crash on a mountaintop, and a lovely Indian girl was the only survivor.

As Mr. Dmytryk and Anna waited in the hotel suite, the bedroom door opened and Spencer Tracy stepped out, and before she could react he embraced her in a bear hug, lifted Anna off the ground, turned to Mr. Dmytryk, and said, "She's the one."

The script called for Tracy to carry her down the mountain—all ninety-eight pounds—and that was it.

Sean Connery

Wolf Mankowitz, a writer, recommended Connery for the first James Bond movie, *Dr. No*. The producers Harry Saltzman and Cubby Broccoli interviewed Connery in their offices and offered him the part, without a screen test.

Other actors considered were James Mason (who thought the part was his but his fee was too high; he was Ian Fleming's choice), Trevor Howard, Richard Burton, and Roger Moore.

Connery was eventually asked to do a screen test after all, after having been told the part was his. The test wasn't for him, he was assured, but to help with the selection of his leading lady. What he didn't know was United Artists was unhappy with Connery as Bond and that twenty other actors were being auditioned.

The test merely confirmed the belief of both producers that Connery was it. None of the other actors measured up to him. But United Artists still didn't agree. A telegram from their New York office to the producers said, "See if you can do better."

Sean Connery went on to play James Bond in seven more Bond films.

Cybill Shepherd

George Cukor was a Hollywood movie director who almost everyone acknowledged as a master of film comedy. He was especially successful working with talented and beautiful actresses, and when Cybill was able to get an audition with him she felt honored. The movie was *Travels with My Aunt.* After the audition, Mr. Cukor said, "That was a really bad reading. Why don't you take it home and study it. You can come back and try tomorrow."

Cybill worked on it with a friend, Peter Bogdanovich, for three hours, didn't get much sleep that night, and came in to read for Mr. Cukor the next morning. When it was over, Mr. Cukor said, "I'm going to give you some good advice, and if you have any sense, you'll take it. You have no comedic talent, never try it again."

Mae West

New York, 1944: Mike Todd was producing *Catherine the Great* starring Mae West. Bill Browder, an actor in his twenties, got an appointment to audition. He appeared at the theatre, quite presentable in a suit and a tie, joining the horde of actors waiting to audition. To his amazement, almost all the actors were wearing denim pants (this was 1944, when jeans were only worn to go camping or on a ranch).

Up next, Bill walked on to center stage and heard from the darkened house the unmistakable voice of Mae West.

"I don't see anything in him."

Mr. Todd said that he wanted her to hear Bill read.

But Mae West insisted.

"I don't see anything in him."

A light went on in Bill's brain. The jeans! They were more crotch-hugging than the trousers he was wearing.

Bill never got to read.

Howard Rodman

Television is a youth-oriented medium, run by relatively young people. Not just actors (especially women), but also behind-the-scenes people and writers often complain of age discrimination.

Howard, a highly respected Hollywood writer, was asked in his sixties by a very young television executive:

"And what have you done, Mr. Howard?"

"Before or after you were born?" the writer inquired.

Ken Howard

The movie *The Way We Were* happened simply this way: Producer Ray Stark asked playwright Arthur Laurents to come up with a story for Barbra Streisand. Arthur did. A politically activist student in the thirties falls for and weds a golden-haired WASP type. You know, opposites attract. A few stars were considered like Ryan O'Neal, but the equation was not right until Ken Howard's name was brought up.

Ken was out in L.A. shooting the musical *1776*, reprising the role he played on Broadway. He was perfect for the tall blond WASP type to play opposite Barbra. An audition was set up.

This may have been one of the oddest auditions ever. It was to be played on a tennis court . . . yes, a tennis court. It was a doubles match, Barbra and Ken vs. Arthur and ballet star Nora Kaye.

All was going well until a stunning girl came by to pick up Ken. According to Arthur, "Barbra froze." Later, Barbra said there was no sexual attraction between her and Ken and, of course, that would undermine the film. Ken was out of the picture, Redford, in.

Rod Steiger

Rod, an Academy Award winner playing the southern sheriff in the movie *In the Heat of the Night*, recently went in to see one of those studio VP's with the Armani suit and the greasy hair.

He says, "Oh, Mr. Steiger, what an honor! Tell me, can you do a southern accent?"

Skip Hinnant

At an ad agency, they are seeing actors for a commercial. Skip and another actor are auditioning. They read the copy in front of several ad men. They finish. One of the ad men says, "Brighter! Funny, funny!"

The actors read the copy once more. "No, no, make it funnier and brighter, okay?"

Again, the actors have a go at it. An ad man shakes his head, gets up and says, "Guys, funny, brighter and funnier!"

Skip looks at the younger ad man, "Are you the writer?"

Puzzled, he answers, "Why, yes."

"*You're* the writer . . . *you* make it funny."

Jose Ferrer

Bill Browder had worked with Jose Ferrer for a year in the touring company of *Othello*. A year or so later, when he was casting for *Cyrano*, Bill was sure of an inside track. As he stood in a crowd of actors in his outer office, Jose walked out, saw him in the back of the mob and called him. By name! He asked Bill to step inside. Sure of employment, Bill walked proudly through the horde, feeling their envy as he entered the inner sanctum. Once inside, Jose introduced him to the director, Mel Ferrer, and the others in the office. He then turned to Bill and said, "We're starving. Would you run down to the deli?"

Harry Hamlin

Steven Spielberg was casting for the two leads for his movie *Raiders of the Lost Ark*, and Harry and Stephanie Zimbalist were there to audition. They hadn't ever worked together before. The place: Lucasfilm's kitchen, oddly enough. Mr. Spielberg came in, greeted them, and explained what he wanted them to do. They were to make a chocolate cake . . . all the ingredients needed were to be found in the kitchen, then he excused himself to make a call.

The two very surprised actors admitted to each other that baking cakes was not what they did; nevertheless, they went at it. They found the makings pretty easily: milk, butter and eggs in the fridge, the cake mix in the cabinets, etc. Without too much trouble, the cake came out fine. They were very proud of themselves, admiring their culinary skills, when Mr. Spielberg returned.

He praised them for their efforts and thanked them for coming in, adding that they were not exactly what he was looking for. Puzzled, they looked at the cake, feeling they had fulfilled their task. Mr. Spielberg explained, "I felt you two didn't work well together." By now, Harry was mystified, till Mr. Spielberg said, "You see, we *taped* the whole thing."

Sally Kirkland

Auditioning for the legendary director George Abbott for the musical *Flora the Red Menace*, Sally sang and was about to read when she heard "Thank you."

Sally: "But I haven't read yet."

Mr. Abbott: "Thank you."

Sally: "You don't understand . . . I spent five hundred dollars for singing lessons and coaching for this audition . . . I want this . . . this means a lot to me . . . it's my first audition!"

Mr. Abbott: "And your last."

Sally walked off stage, closed the door, and through the door screamed, "I'm going to be the biggest star you ever saw, George Abbott!"

Vivian Vance

One of her first auditions when Vivian arrived in New York from Albuquerque, New Mexico, was for Eva Le Gallienne's Civic Repertory Theatre. Miss Le Gallienne did not let Vivian know the result of the audition immediately . . . days passed . . . weeks.

Vivian couldn't sleep, couldn't eat, and she felt she had wasted the money the town of Albuquerque had raised specifically for her big trip to New York City.

Finally the notice came, she opened the envelope. "So sorry to inform you . . . may we suggest you immediately return home."

Paul Reiser

At a meeting with one network executive and his assistant, Paul, with his manager, was pitching a story idea. In the middle of it, the executive got up from behind his desk and walked out of the office saying, "Keep talking," and disappeared.

Joe Elic

A character actor for a number of years, Joe, while waiting outside of the office auditioning for a commercial, found himself sitting next to this man who seemed nervous.

Man: "Do you think they'll be very long?"

Joe: "I don't know . . . why?"

Man: "I'm a doctor. I've got patients waiting . . . this is the sixth audition I've been in on, and I haven't gotten one yet."

Joe, who actually auditioned 324 times before he got his first commercial, looked at him and fought this overwhelming urge to pick him up and throw him out of the window.

Louis Zorich

One of the more exciting events one particular year in New York was the announcement that John Whiting's play *The Devils* was going to be produced on Broadway, and the director was the internationally known Michael Cacoyannis, the man responsible for the long running Off-Broadway hit *Trojan Women*. Everyone in New York wanted to be in *The Devils*, and especially to have the opportunity to work with a director of such stature. Fortunately, I was able to get an audition and I never worked harder. I was determined to get the part.

I stepped out on the stage and began reading, when Mr. Cacoyannis stopped me in the middle of the very first line and read it for me. He then asked me to repeat it. I did. I proceeded to the next line and he stopped me again, gave me a line reading, and if I didn't have the proper inflection he made me repeat it until I read it exactly the way he did. This went on and on and on. I don't believe I ever got through the speech. I, the actor Louis Zorich, left the stage . . . literally, speechless!

Hy Anzel

Hy relates a story about an older character actor named Florenz Ames who comes to this audition where the casting person was barely twenty years old, totally inexperienced and with an attitude that Mr. Ames picked up on immediately.

Casting person: "Your name?"

Mr. Ames: "Edwin Booth."

Casting person: "And what have you done, Mr. Booth?"

Mr. Ames rattles off a long list of credits which include *Our American Cousin* (from the 1850s), *Uncle Tom's Cabin*, etc., and he adds, "I've been dead for sixty-five years," and walks out.

Austin Pendleton

1. Austin was auditioning for a movie with a slouched-in-his-chair Robert De Niro, who was hostile, condescending, and muttering his lines. Frustrated in his attempt to play the scene with him, Austin, feeling resentful and angry, began an interior monologue as he was doing the scene . . . "You arrogant bastard, Al Pacino's a better actor than you . . . so is Dustin Hoffman . . . you're nothing . . . you're terrible at comedy and your last three films were flops."

2. Before auditioning for Brian De Palma, the movie director's secretary informed Austin, "Mr. De Palma is in a bad mood today."

With that in mind, Austin read . . . and as he did, De Palma, at his desk, was shuffling papers, opening and slamming shut drawers, banging books. Austin, meanwhile, struggled bravely to keep his cool and managed somehow to get through it.

De Palma: "Finished?" Austin nodded and left.

Cutting through Central Park after the horror-of-an-audition, he began to scream, "Listen to me, you chicken-shit De Palma, fuck you! . . . fuck you! . . . fuck you! . . . fuck you!"

Frank Langella

After Frank had auditioned for *Dave*, a movie directed by Ivan Reitman, for the part of the scheming chief of staff, he was told he was perfect. Months later, Frank got the part. One day on the set he asked Mr. Reitman why he had waited so long to tell him. Mr. Reitman replied, "I was looking for someone better."

Anonymous

This actor was brought in to audition for a narration of a documentary about archeology. With the producer he viewed the film, went over the twelve-page script a few times, and then taped it three times.

It was one of the longest auditions that he could recall, but he felt the producer knew exactly what she needed and he was sure he gave her what she wanted.

After some two straight hours they took a break, when she asked him if he knew of Lowell Thomas, the most famous narrator of his day. The actor nodded.

"That's who I really want for this."

Goldie Hawn

Goldie was auditioning for the Broadway musical *Li'l Abner*, and its creator, Al Capp, was there in person seeing potential actresses for Daisy Mae, the female lead. After Goldie read, Capp began to direct her, "Walk over there, now pull up your dress so I can see your legs." She did.

Sitting, wearing an open robe, Capp put his right leg up on the couch and leaned back. Goldie gasped. Capp's right leg was wooden. Goldie was transfixed.

Capp said, "You'll never get anywhere in this business, go back home and marry that Jewish dentist like your mother said you should."

Goldie replied, "I will, I can't take a job like this . . . and I'm late for my other job." Capp threw her a twenty-dollar bill for a cab and off she went to the World's Fair, where she danced the can-can.

William Fichtner

Fichtner was up for a TV pilot, *Checkered Flag*. After reading again and again for the role of an auto racer, he truly felt he was going to get it. But then his agent called, and said he wasn't "eight o'clock."

"What the hell does that mean?" asked Fichtner.

"The network said you're too intense for the family slot, the eight o'clock time . . . but you're right for late-evening heavier drama."

Mike Fischetti

On a break making a movie in Hollywood, Mike, an actor who has done a lot of work over the years, decided to take a walk around the lot. He spotted a parked limo and a few men in conversation. One of the men opened the back door of the limo, snapped his fingers, and a small dog jumped out and on command sat and barked, "yip, yip."

The other man looked on and shook his head while the other man signaled the dog to get into the limo, then signaled for a larger dog to hop out. This one did the same but barked, "arf, arf."

The man shook his head—"arf, arf" hopped back into the limo. The third dog, again on command, leaped out and "woof, woofed," and he too was turned down. The last dog came out with a "grrr, grrr." He too was rejected.

Mike, watching all this, left thinking of his career, and of the movie *My Life as a Dog*.

George Abbott

1. Donald Saddler, who worked with Mr. Abbott a number of years as an associate director and choreographer, tells a story about assisting him at musical auditions. Frequently, singers auditioning would ask for a chair on stage, whereupon Donald would hear Mr. Abbott, next to him, grunt.

A particular singer got her chair, sat in it, got up, walked around while singing. In the middle of the song, Mr. Abbott stopped her and said, "Just sing the song, dear, we'll stage it later."

2. Mr. Abbott has done it all—actor, playwright, director, producer—and he was at it well into his nineties when he directed his last play, *Broadway*. It was in the fifties when he was seeing people for the musical *Fiorello*, and on this particular day, a young man was auditioning with his song. Mr. Abbott, who sat in the back of the theatre, cut him off with, "I can't hear you." The young man replied, "Well, could you move down a little?"

The young man was not in *Fiorello*.

Kay Thompson

Kay, who in the early days of radio in New York sang with the well-known Mills Brothers and later with Fred Waring, was so successful that CBS offered her her own show, *Kay Thompson and Co.* It flopped, so Kay went out to Hollywood, where she got to work in various capacities at MGM with the producer Arthur Freed, who was responsible for a number of the great MGM musicals, like *On the Town* and *Singing in the Rain*.

Kay not only served as vocal coach to stars like Judy Garland and Lena Horne but also brought considerable songwriting talents to bear at the studio, in addition to being prominently featured in the musical *Cover Girl*. Frequently, she would audition for Arthur Freed singing her own numbers. After one audition Freed said, "Kay, you sang that great, you are terrific . . . now who can we get to sing it?"

Frankie Faison

Faison shares this story:

I was auditioning for the movie *Ragtime*, for the supporting role of Zeke, one of the members of the gang. After giving (in my mind) an outstanding audition, I felt I was the only one to play the role. The next day my agent called to tell me they were offering me the part. I was excited beyond belief, for this was a big-budget film. The production office contacted me for my wardrobe fittings, they sent me the script and gave me my start date.

Then I got this strange call from my agent: production wants to bring in all four gang members to see if they all fit in the period car they're using. When I show up, I find the gang of four is now five. They had us all sit in the car in various combinations and positions, but it was painfully clear; there was room for only four, not five, in the car. I got very nervous, I'm very large and well-built, and the others, medium. I heard one of us would be out of a job . . . and I figured me.

But when we began filming, I discovered it wasn't me but another actor who had already been cast.

Nothing, even when you have the job and a signed contract, is guaranteed in this business. What we thought was about fitting in a period car was really about musical chairs. Who knows when the music will stop and you will be left without a chair?

Sue Mengers

Sue, for a time, was one of the most powerful agents in Hollywood, handling clients like Barbra Streisand, Faye Dunaway, and Gene Hackman. Legend has it that whenever young unknowns came to see her about representation, Sue's line was, "Come back to see me when you're a star!"

Leo McCarey

Veteran Hollywood producer/director Leo McCarey had a script about Adam and Eve that he felt had a lot of possibilities. With his reputation, every actor and actress wanted to be part of McCarey's project.

A big name from the silent movies era came to see McCarey about playing Eve. She walked in "dressed as an aging ingenue."

McCarey sighed and said, "It's true I'm working on a new version of *Adam and Eve*—but not with the original cast."

Peter Lorre

Peter, though born in Hungary, had his biggest success in German films, namely *M*, directed by Fritz Lang, in which he played a psychopathic child murderer with eye-popping intensity.

He subsequently came to Hollywood and met this producer who promised Peter a part in his film but then reneged on his promise. Peter, hoping to get the part back, turned up at the producer's office. One small problem. Peter could barely speak a word of English. All he could do was stand there and stare steadily at the producer with those huge globular eyes of his.

There was silence, only those eyes. They scared the hell out of the producer so that he yelled out to Peter, "Stop staring at me like this, you can have your part!"

Charlton Heston

One would think Heston's majestic stature or riveting presence would have landed him the role of Moses in Cecil B. DeMille's remake of the epic *The Ten Commandments*. Not so.

It seems that it was his broken nose . . . the one he got playing football in college. Mr. DeMille, in his research, discovered that the statue of Moses by Michelangelo has his nose broken in the same place as Heston's!

Lucille Ball

There was a time, in the "good old days" of Hollywood, when if you were beautiful and could dance you could be a Goldwyn girl. There were quite a few, Lucille being one of them. With so many girls, Lucy felt she had to do something to separate herself from the other chorines.

It just so happened that Goldwyn was having a session with his writers on the lot. Lucy went into action. She drove her car up next to that building and started to blow the car horn. She would not let up. She was determined to see Goldwyn. From out of the second floor balcony stormed Goldwyn. He peered down to see who the hell was making all that racket.

Lucy looked up at the pissed-off Goldwyn with her oh-so-sweet little-girly smile and said, "Can the writers come out and play with me now?"

Burt Reynolds

Sean Connery was becoming weary of playing James Bond, which made the producers very antsy and moved them quickly to find another actor for Bond. Guy Hamilton, who directed *Goldfinger* in 1964 and who was to do the next *Bond* picture, happened to be watching a talk show on TV and saw someone he felt was Bond.

He got on the phone with "Cubby" Broccoli, one of the producers, and said, "I found James Bond." He got together with Broccoli, who agreed with him, and they went to the casting director at United Artists with the idea.

"He's just a stunt guy. . . . he's going nowhere at all." He talked them out of the next James Bond . . . Burt Reynolds.

Roland Young

The time was 1937 and Broadway had a very successful play called *The Last of Mrs. Chesney*. The star of the play and the reason for its wonderful reception was Roland.

One of the studios in Hollywood bought the rights to the play and arranged for Roland to come out to L.A. to star in the filming of it. Roland took the train out west, only to discover that "he was not the right type to play the role that he had created."

Luchino Visconti

Visconti (*Rocco and His Brothers, The Damned, White Nights*), one of the early Italian directors of realism after World War II, preferred to cast people who looked right and who weren't professionals. Film directors like Visconti felt that using actors helped to destroy the illusion that movies are about real people.

Casting for his next movie was under way when an unemployed actor barged into Visconti's office and said, "I know you want nonactors, I am an actor. I'm not working because I can't act. My speech is bad, I'm clumsy, let's face it, I'm terrible . . . so how about hiring me?"

Visconti, at first annoyed, started to laugh at "his act." Sizing him up, he said, "Go to my casting director, tell him I want you to play the part of a terrible actor."

Margaret Cho

The first Asian-American family was about to appear on national TV. Margaret, a stand-up comic, screen-tested for the proposed series. She was treated exceptionally well during the test, especially by Gail, the head producer, who made Margaret feel wanted and needed, dispelling any fears Margaret had since this was a big opportunity for her.

Shortly after, Gail called Margaret . . . the people from the network were worried about Margaret's weight. The pilot was to be shot soon and if she were to star in the series, changes were necessary. Furthermore, the network was "concerned about the fullness of your face."

Margaret's reaction? "I will never forget it, as long as I live."

John Curtis Brown

A friend of John's, a voice-over actor, has specialized for some twenty years in children's voices and parrot voices. He is called in to audition for a parrot voice-over, which he expertly does in a few takes. He is confident he'll get it. He doesn't hear for a week or two, so he calls his agent, who tells him that the client is going with a younger parrot.

Allen Swift

Allen was one of the top voice-over actors in New York for years. One day he was called in to audition for the voice of a fountain pen.

"Regular or ball point?" he asked.

The job was his.

Franklin Cover

Up for a cereal commercial, Franklin found himself sitting at an ad agency muttering, "Four years of Yale drama school and what am I reading for? An *angry* raisin!"

"Stop! He's my agent!"

Chapter Seven

Making an Impression

John Guare

Guare saw many similarities in his plays to those of another playwright, Thornton Wilder. Both dramatists created characters who were eternally hopeful even while living in disturbing times. "In every one of my plays," Guare said, "there is that feeling of, 'If I could only show you who I really am, you would love me totally.'" In Guare's *The House of Blue Leaves*, a young lad seizes the opportunity to do an on-the-spot performance for an uncle who has some showbiz connections. Well, why not? Unfortunately, the uncle doesn't take too kindly to the boy's efforts, and he lets his feelings be known to his parents. "You never told me you had a mentally retarded child."

"Yes, that happened to me," Mr. Guare said with a smile. "And that's what all my plays are about, that child in all of us who cries: 'Pick me! Pick me!' Which is why I keep writing for the theater. The audition never ends."

Bruce Willis

Glenn Gordon Caron wrote the TV pilot *Moonlighting* with Cybill Shepherd in mind for the character Maddie Hayes, who becomes a partner in a detective agency run by a character named David Addison, who is cocky and sexually aggressive with humor and charm. Some three thousand actors responded to the casting call. Cybill felt there had to be a chemistry between the two leads, Maddie and David, and the style of the show was quick give-and-take, overlapping dialogue, and, most importantly, sexual tension had to exist between the two.

Given the nature and thrust of the show, Cybill had casting approval, and when the list of actors being considered had narrowed down to about six, Cybill had to see them. No one seemed quite right. Bruce came in next. He had a smirk, a devil-may-care attitude. He seemed to avoid her, not making eye contact with her at all, relating more to the producers in the room and he didn't do what the other auditioning actors had done, he didn't flatter her. Still, Cybill felt a chemistry between her and Bruce. She told Glenn, "He's the one."

But the network saw Bruce playing "heavies," not leading men, and they weren't impressed with his slim professional background: a bartender in New York. They were looking for a name actor.

Cybill was determined to convince the network that Bruce was right for the part. She agreed to screen test with him. Just before the scene was about to begin, Bruce looked at Cybill and said, "I can't concentrate, you're too beautiful."

That did it for Cybill and the network.

John Malkovich

John, on getting to play Biff with Dustin Hoffman in *Death of a Salesman*:

"Well, so many famous people, I mean *stars*, were shaking in their boots waiting to read with Dustin. I wasn't scared. I just went for him and started flinging him around. He loved it. He wanted people who'd challenge him. I'm not the nervous type. Dustin's an excellent actor, but I've worked with some great actors all my life."

Orson Welles

Joseph Cotten, in his early years, decided to go into radio in New York City. He found out all the names of producers and directors. The practice was to go to their offices and wait for an audition. Knowles Entrekin's office at CBS on Madison Avenue was the big one. Knowles was the director of CBS radio dramas, and actors got cast by "looking in" on Knowles.

At one of these auditions, Joseph met another actor, a young man named Orson Welles. Knowles introduced them, since Orson and Joseph had "looked in" simultaneously, and during their chat, Orson put the contents of his pipe in the wastepaper basket . . . and set the office afire.

At a later time, Knowles remarked, "That young man certainly left an impression."

Later, that same young man created an even *greater* impression with the sensational radio drama that caused some listeners to panic in the streets . . . *The War of the Worlds.*

Linda Blair

William Friedkin, director of the film *The Exorcist*, was having problems finding the right actress for the part of Regan, the girl who was possessed. One of the actresses he interviewed was Linda Blair, who was twelve years old at the time. Friedkin asked her if she had read *The Exorcist.*

"Yes."

"What's it about?"

"A little girl who gets possessed by the devil and does a lot of bad things."

"What sort of bad things?"

"She pushes a guy out the window and masturbates with a crucifix."

"What does that mean?"

"It's like jerking off, isn't it?"

"Yeah, do you know about jerking off?"

"Oh, sure."
"Do you do that?"
"Yeah, don't you?"
She got the role.

French Stewart

The original character of Harry in the TV series *Third Rock from the Sun* was initially conceived to be a "large physical guy." French, a rather small, slender actor, made them rewrite the character after his audition, which was clinched by the way he rubbed his angora sweater against his face.

Henry Fonda

In the late twenties, early thirties, an actor friend of Fonda's, Glenn Anders, heard that Leonard Sillman had put together a revue called *Low and Behold* to be done in New York. Anders invited Fonda to accompany him to the Algonquin Hotel. He called Sillman on the house phone.

"Leonard," he said, "I know an actor who needs a job."

Fonda went up to Sillman's one-bedroom apartment.

"Do you sing?" Sillman asked.

"Nope."

"Do you dance?'

"Nope."

"Well, what *do* you do?"

Fonda said, "I do imitations of babies from one week to one year."

"Well, can you do one of them now?"

Fonda then pantomimed a man driving a car and simultaneously changing a baby's diaper. Within minutes, Sillman was lying across an armchair collapsing with laughter.

Low and Behold was a big hit, with Fonda and Imogene Coca being singled out for particular praise.

John Cassavetes

Old friend and classmate Harry Mastergeorge (Mastrogeorge, then) will never forget looking for acting work with John during the days of live television in New York. One day, John, Harry, and Jerry Stiller approached the receptionist to a producer and asked to see him. They were told that he was not in.

John, visibly upset and angry, said to her that it was impossible because they had, moments ago, seen him getting out of the elevator. As Harry recalls, John suddenly grabbed his chest, gasped for air, and fell to the floor. Everyone was stunned.

The receptionist, in shock, ran into the office and hurried back with the producer. He got to John just as John jumped to his feet and said, "Do you know how long I've been trying to see you?"

The producer, by now furious at John, exploded, "Get the hell out of here, and don't you ever come back!!!"

As he was leaving, John pulled out some of his photos, flung them up in the air and said, "Here . . . here . . . in case you need me!!"

Robert Blake

Brandon Tartikoff at one time was a very successful NBC-TV head. One day Blake rushes into his office dressed as a priest saying, "Name me the biggest thing that ever hit the world?" Recognizing Blake from *Baretta* and *In Cold Blood*, Brandon caught off-guard, blurts out, "*60 Minutes*? . . . aah, Walt Disney?"

Blake sits there hoping for the right answer. Brandon, playing the game, waits for an inspired idea. . . . "Ok, who, what?"

"None other than J.C.—Jesus Christ—who's been around forever, and I have this great idea. You see, there's this priest in East L.A. whose flock is in the barrio. *Hell Town* is the name. I play the Catholic priest. Do you like it?"

Brandon did. The pilot was a big hit. The series and J.C.—Jesus Christ—were only around for seventeen episodes.

Fifi D'Orsay

Soon after *Company* opened in New York City, Hal Prince and Stephen Sondheim went to work on their next project, *Follies*, a bittersweet valentine to the great musical traditions of the past.

They assembled a first-rate cast, including Alexis Smith and John McMartin, and Yvonne De Carlo was logically cast as the aging movie star. And there was Fifi D'Orsay, a well-known musical-theatre performer from the twenties who made such an impression at the audition that Sondheim wrote the show-stopping song "Ah, Paris" especially for her.

John Belushi

For his *Saturday Night* audition, John chose to do a role he loved and was good at, the samurai pool hustler; his model was the Japanese film actor Toshiro Mifune. His hair was styled like Mifune and for his pool cue John had a stick from his closet.

The audition hall was mobbed, there were actors everywhere—staircases, hallways, all hoping to be part of Lorne Michaels' TV comedy repertory company. So many that they were falling behind, way behind, hours and hours behind. John, waiting for four hours, got impatient, frustrated, then angry, very angry.

John began to pace up and down the crowded halls downstairs shouting obscenities, brandishing his weapon-like cue stick. His rantings were heard upstairs in the audition room causing fear and trepidation prompting one of the writers to say, "He'd better get hired or he'll kill someone."

Finally John was ushered into the room. They expected the worst—mayhem, carnage—but John shrewdly outwitted them. He was a pussy, he prowled around the imaginary pool table, making sounds as he surveyed his prey, scratching himself here and there, totally mesmerizing his captive audience.

It was not what they had expected. It was a "winning performance, a *tour de force*."

Abe Vigoda

Abe Vigoda shares this story:

All my life I've been an athlete and almost, when younger, a champion handball player. While living in Los Angeles, I'd jog three to five miles a day. One morning jogging, my agent calls about a new series called *Barney Miller*, saying, "Go there at once."

Well, I was tired and exhausted . . . I must have run five miles that morning. I said, "I have to go home and take a shower.

"No, no, no, go right now to Studio City, you're very right for it, they know you from *The Godfather*, they want to see you."

"With my shorts?"

"Go!"

Danny Arnold and Ted Flicker, the producers, look at me, I look at them, they look at me again. "You look tired."

"Of course I'm tired, I jogged five miles this morning, I'm exhausted."

"Yeah, yeah, tell me, you look like you have hemorrhoids."

"What are you, a doctor or a producer?"

Abe went on to play Fish, the tired detective who was always going to the toilet.

Andy Griffith

Andy, who has won a Grammy as a singer, loves to tell the story of how his voice was once panned at an audition as "brilliantly over-pleasant." He turned to joke writing instead.

Walter Brennan

Howard Hawks, directing a film titled *Barbary Coast*, took a chance with an extra on the movie with hardly any experience. A part that was open seemed to fit Walter, according to someone connected to the movie.

Walter came to see Howard to read.

Walter: "With or without?"

Howard: "With or without what?"

Walter: "Teeth."

Howard: "Without teeth?"

Walter removed his dentures and read the scene with Howard. The four-day part turned into six weeks and an Academy Award nomination for Walter.

Morris Robinson

This has to be the most remarkable audition story I (Louis Zorich) have ever come across. Picture this: Standing six feet three inches tall and weighing in at three hundred pounds, Morris Robinson, a former All-American football player from the Citadel, earned a high salary as a sales manager before he began to get serious about a music career—in opera.

Morris happened to have a God-given voice, a very low basso. After taking some weekend classes at the New England Conservatory, he went to Boston University's Opera Institute on a full scholarship, working at Best Buy for twelve dollars an hour to supplement his stipend there. He sang three years with Boston's Lyric Opera and then tried out for the Metropolitan Opera's young artists' program, singing the bass aria from Mozart's *The Magic Flute*. He had sung only three notes when the conductor, James Levine, said to his aide, "He's hired."

Frances Sternhagen

Sternhagen tells this story:

I taught school for a year after college in a school outside of Boston, and thought I'd try to audition for the Brattle Theatre in Cambridge, not knowing that the Brattle was going to close down the following year. So I managed to get someone to arrange an audition for me with the producer, who took me down to a little room in the basement. The producer was a young man with blond hair, spectacles, and a tweed jacket with leather patches, like an Alan Bennett character, and he had a Groton-Harvard accent; i.e., he sounded a little like Franklin D. Roosevelt.

When he sat down, he pulled out his pipe and began to fill it, and told me to begin. I had five very different pieces: Chekhov, Shakespeare, Shaw, Williams, and Wilder. As I started, the producer lit his pipe. My husband, years later, said, "Beware the director who smokes a pipe, he's more interested in keeping it lit than in anything that's going on on stage." So, there I was, going through my paces as he puffed, tamped, and lit match after match. I finished. He said in his best F.D.R. voice, "Ms. Sternhagen, if you want to be an actress, give up teaching; you do everything as if you were leading the Girl Scouts onto the hockey field."

Trevor Howard

Noel Coward wrote the film script *Brief Encounter*, which was based on one of his short plays from *Tonight at 8:30*. Having casting approval, Noel was a stickler for casting correctly as opposed to using names. Celia Johnson was set for the female lead, but her co-star wasn't. In their search, producers Ronald Neame and David Lean, while looking at the rushes of the film *The Way to the Stars*, in which Trevor appeared, suddenly felt, "That's him!" They ran the same footage for Mr. Coward. "Look no further," he said.

The scene: an aerodrome; a plane came over the field and did a victory roll. Trevor, the actor, looked up and said: "Lineshoot." That's all.

"I'll never forget it," said David Lean, "how he looked, and how he said it."

One word . . . just one word.

Barnard Hughes

Hughes shares this story:

I always loved the theatre. Growing up in New York, my parents went all the time, so I saw everything when I was a kid. I was highly critical of everything, the actors, especially the young ones—I thrashed them after the show.

A friend of mine got annoyed at my being so critical of everything. One day I got a postcard saying that a man named Franklin Short had received my letter and that he would be happy to audition me next week with something I prepared, five minutes long.

I didn't know what the hell it was all about, so I showed the mysterious postcard to my friend, Art Nesbit. He said he read about a man forming a Shakespeare company to play schools and colleges and he submitted my name because I was always shooting my mouth off about how much better I was than so-and-so.

I had no idea what the hell an audition was, so I memorized a poem, Pope's "The Dying Christian to His Soul," went down and read it for the old man. He must have been shocked. I got the part.

Iggie Wolfington

Moving back to New York from L.A., one of his first auditions was for *Music Man*. Iggie rented the movie, learned the "Shipoopi" number, and worked on it. He auditioned for its creator, Meredith Willson, and the choreographer, Oona White—everybody but the backstage doorman.

Not hearing anything, he took a job touring in a show and now and then would check in with his answering service. Six different agents had called for him about the *Music Man*. Wow, he thought, he must be hot for this part.

At the audition, backstage was a mob of actors waiting their turn, every shape and size: tall, short, skinny, round, which made Iggie wonder, "They're not waiting for me, they're just looking for anyone."

Iggie's turn came up. He sang a little bit and started to do bell kicks: put one foot up in the air and then kick up the other foot to meet it, clicking your heels.

That's when Iggie got the job.

Dan Aykroyd

Producer Lorne Michaels was seeing talent for a new TV show, *Saturday Night,* based in New York, done live by a company of young comedic performers. When word got out, hundreds of people showed up at the Nola rehearsal studios on the west side.

Auditions were held over a two-day period to accommodate the overflowing number of people who were sprawled everywhere in the hallways and staircases. Each appointment was for ten minutes, but they were running very late. People were kept waiting for hours and the situation was getting tense.

At one point, in a break, a man charged into the audition room, sporting a derby and an umbrella along with an attache case. He fixed his stare at Lorne and the writers sitting there, and, you might say, vented: "I've been waiting out there for three hours, but I'm not hanging around anymore . . . I've got a plane to catch . . . gentlemen, you've had your chance!" And he dashed out.

Everyone had the feeling of "What the hell was that?"

Lorne said, "Oh, that was Dan Aykroyd, he's probably going to do the show."

Imogene Coca

Coca, the rubber-faced comedienne who teamed with Sid Caesar on NBC-TV's hugely successful *Show of Shows* for five years in the early fifties, though born into a show business family, had some rough times early on in her career. For years she bounced from show to show but finally got her lucky break.

Coca, who once said she never had any interest in comedy, stumbled into it when she auditioned for the revue *New Faces of 1934.* Trying to stay warm in a cold theatre, Coca borrowed a man's camel-hair coat that was several sizes too big and began clowning around on stage: a fan dance with flapping ends. The producer, Leonard Sillman, saw it, was impressed. Coca and the coat were in the show.

Carol Burnett

The Garry Moore TV variety show, originating out of New York in the early fifties, was looking for fresh talent. Carol, young and fresh, at her audition played the part of a shy, inexperienced girl doing an audition.

Barely into her song, Ken Welch, accompanying her on the piano, launched into a long series of elaborate arpeggios. Carol fell silent and watched him, transfixed. After he had finished the passage, she did not pick up the song, but now completely herself, went to the piano and said in a funny, but absolutely sincere way:

"O-o-oh, that's wonderful."

She was booked on the show that week.

Robin Williams

Scott Marshall, son of Garry Marshall, the producer of the seventies hit TV show *Happy Days*, gave his dad an idea for one of the episodes. What if an alien dropped in on Milwaukee?

A number of actors were seen for the part of the alien. Among them was then- unknown actor Robin Williams, who came in to the audition in a T-shirt and rainbow suspenders. He was asked to give "some idea of how you'd sit down as an extra-terrestrial."

Robin, quiet for a moment, crossed the room to the couch and sat on his head. The place exploded with laughter. The episode with Robin was aired and caused a sensation. A series was subsequently created and starred him and his alien character, Mork from Ork.

Bob Fosse

Frank Milton said he auditioned for Fosse over and over again and he always used to come running down the aisle and up on stage to tell him how great he was and then say, "If only there was something in the show for you."

David O. Selznick

Hollywood producer Selznick created a publicity whirlwind when he announced that he was initiating an unprecedented search for an unknown actress to play the part of Scarlett O'Hara in his forthcoming epic *Gone with the Wind*. At the same time, he was testing such established stars as Jean Arthur, Joan Bennett, and Paulette Goddard. Seemingly, every actress in Hollywood and New York was hungry to play Scarlett.

One actress, after being turned down in an audition in New York, followed George Cukor, its director, to Atlanta, where she got on the train and searched every car to find Cukor, who was told about her by his aides. She "forcibly held on the platform" while Cukor was able to escape by climbing up on the coal car.

Katharine Hepburn

Along with every other female star in the world, Hepburn coveted the role of Scarlett O'Hara. Selznick ended their interview quickly saying, "I can't imagine Gable chasing you for ten years!"

Lucille Ball

One of the auditioning hopefuls for the part of Scarlett O'Hara was Lucille, who at the time was a young unknown actress working for RKO studios. On the way to the audition at Selznick-International Studios, she got caught in the rain, and she was drying herself off before the fireplace in the producer's office when Selznick walked in.

He gave her a scene to read. After he thanked her, she realized she had done the whole audition on her knees.

Years later, Lucy and husband, Desi Arnaz, bought the Selznick Studios for their TV series *I Love Lucy*. Out of nostalgia, or maybe revenge, Lucy chose for herself . . . Selznick's old office.

Anonymous

At the Selznick-International Studios came a huge packing case with a sign on it. "Open at once." As the secretary opened the case, a young woman jumped out and dashed into Selznick's office.

She started to strip while reciting Scarlett O'Hara's lines.

Vivien Leigh

It's a well-known fact that it was David O. Selznick's brother Myron, an agent, who brought Vivien on the movie set to watch the burning of Atlanta. Up to that evening, no Scarlett had been found, so, of necessity, three different stand-ins were used in silhouette against the background of flames. David, watching the action with his executives, was approached by Myron, "Hey, genius, I'd like you to meet your Scarlett O'Hara."

She was given a "cold reading" on the spot with the director George Cukor and later was screen-tested. But there were attendant problems. She was not a well-known star, and she was "foreign," coming from England. Would Southern women in America accept her? Also she was under contract with the British film producer Alexander Korda. Vivien was convinced she wasn't going to get it.

At his Christmas Day party, Cukor matter-of-factly told Vivien that the casting was finally settled. Fearing the worst, she said, "It must be a big relief to you."

"Oh, yes," Cukor said, and to not prolong her anxiety, added, "I guess we're stuck with you."

Kieran Culkin

Burr Steers, director of the movie *Igby Goes Down*, was auditioning teenage boys for the key role and went through a number of hopefuls, when Kieran, the younger brother of Macaulay (who starred in *Home Alone* and the sequel), came skipping into the room, took one look at Burr and said, "You look like shit."

That was it. Burr needed a brash kid for the part. He got him.

Nehemiah Persoff

Persoff tells this story:

Several years ago I went to Fox to read for *L.A. Law* for the part of a mohel . . . one who performs circumcisions. I always resent auditions, especially when there is such a body of work on film that they can see . . . but since they're uncertain—I'll help them out. I put on a black suit and hat I wore as a rabbi in *Magnum P.I.*

When I entered the room, someone asked me if I always dress that way. I nodded and offhandedly said, "Sorry I'm late, I was out on a job."

"What kind of job?" They asked.

"I'm a mohel, I had a circumcision."

"You're a mohel!" Turning to the casting director, "I thought he was an actor."

"Well, I am an actor, but it's such an uncertain business, I have to do moheling on the side."

Terribly impressed, someone asked if he wouldn't mind reading. Persoff agreed and make a few script changes . . . and as I left and was about to get in my car, the author ran up to me, "Excuse me, rabbi, is there anything in the script that strikes you as wrong?"

Of course, Persoff played the mohel . . . masterfully.

Yul Brynner

For Richard Rodgers, finding the right actor for the king in *The King and I* was becoming frustrating, since names like Rex Harrison and Alfred Drake were not available. Auditions were held. A balding Asian-looking man with a guitar sat down, glowered at Rodgers, and began "wailing an unintelligible song." A king was crowned—Yul Brynner.

Jayne Mansfield

1. Jayne tried to convince studio boss Darryl F. Zanuck to pick her over Marilyn Monroe for the lead in *The Seven Year Itch* (1955). When she didn't get the assignment, Jayne moaned, "He probably didn't even see the chest—I mean the *test*!"

2. Jayne allegedly won her first TV acting job when she simply wrote her measurements on a piece of paper and had them delivered to the producer.

Wendy Hiller

Wendy, the noted English actress who incidentally was the Eliza Doolittle in the movie *Pygmalion* with Leslie Howard, was at this particular time in America "doing a terrible something" when she received the script for the movie *Sons and Lovers*, based on the autobiographical novel by D. H. Lawrence. With her agent she went to see the producer—a meeting at which she spoke up loud and clear. She pointed out that whoever the writer was, he or she had failed to grasp the essentials of Lawrence's story and, in effect, they had better get their act together. She watched her agent getting smaller in his chair, "all scrunched up," and on leaving the producer's office wondered aloud what his trouble might have been. Well, he thought she wanted to do the film. She did—and she still did. The poor man was obliged to explain that, if you want the part, you never, ever criticize anything in Hollywood. Wendy Hiller was amazed, she couldn't believe that inaccuracies of the most glaring kind should pass without protest. His reply was, "No, you just don't say these things."

But she had, and she got the part.

Jed Harris

In the late twenties Jed was the sensation of Broadway, directing and producing several consecutive hits. He lost a fortune in the crash of 1929 and inevitably his mind turned to Hollywood, the only place relatively unaffected by the

Depression. He arranged to have some mutual friends intro-
duce him to Louis B. Mayer as a potential MGM producer.

"How much do you want a week?" L. B. came right to
the point.

"First tell me how much you get," said Jed, thus terminat-
ing the job interview.

Chevy Chase

In 1974, Dick Ebersole was hired by the NBC president,
Herb Schlosser, to put together a new live weekend comedy
from New York. It turned out to be the *Saturday Night Live*
show, which changed the face of television comedy. It was
brash, irreverent, and topical. He got Lorne Michaels to
produce it.

A talent search was started. It led to improv clubs like
Chicago and Toronto's Second City, the Groundlings in L.A.,
and the National Lampoon's *Lemmings* in New York.

Chevy was seen in the *Lemmings* show by Dick and Lorne,
and after dinner one night the three went walking in the
rain, going from awning to awning. Chevy runs ahead about
two hundred feet, goes into a pothole, does a complete ass
over teakettle into this immense pothole and comes out of it
just soaked. He comes back and he and Lorne look at Dick
and say, "Now how could you say no to somebody who was
crazy enough to do that?"

Chevy became a cast member of *Saturday Night Live.*

Tim Conway

Auditioning for a new show before a roomful of network
people was Tim Conway. Yes, *the* Tim Conway, who co-starred
with Harvey Korman on the never-to-be-forgotten *Carol
Burnett Show.* Mr. Conway was a man not ordinarily required
to audition. Yet he's been asked to audition.

Given to "following his playful impulses," Conway, facing the network brass, suddenly went into a serious pose, right hand on forehead, brows knitted, head bowed thinking, thinking, thinking. . . . He went "into his circle"—a term the great actor/director Stanislavsky used to describe a way of going into yourself, to tap into your "inner resources." Mr. Conway held the pose for three minutes without speaking. The network executives sat there . . . not really knowing what to make of it.

Mr. Conway did not get the job, but he felt he made his point.

Mason Adams

It has been told that one of Hollywood's biggest stars and a two- or three-time Oscar winner, when a young actor in New York, would come into an audition for a commercial, take two scripts, mark up one very carefully, which he would use for his audition, and then mark up the other with completely opposite underlinings for the use of whatever hapless actor or actors might follow him.

Frances McDormand

The Coen brothers, Joel and Ethan (*Fargo, Miller's Crossing*), were casting one of their early films, *Blood Simple*, for the role of a young runaway wife. "We looked at a lot of actresses for the part," Joel said. "We called them the 'almost Abbys.'"

When Frances auditioned, she impressed the brothers so much that they asked her to come back later to read with another actor who had already been cast.

She said she couldn't, because her boyfriend was going to be on a soap and she promised she would watch. Joel laughed at the memory, "Nobody ever says something like that when you're starting to offer them a job. We really liked that. It was so guileless—just what we wanted for Abby."

Ed Blake

Ed is auditioning for a commercial that requires an accent. After a few takes the casting person asks Ed, "Do you speak any foreign languages?"

"Four," Ed replies.

"And you do accents, of course?"

"Yes, I do," Ed says.

"Well, that opens up a whole new area of rejection for you."

Davey Burns

Davey, a Broadway fixture for many years (*The Music Man, Hello Dolly, A Funny Thing Happened on the Way to the Forum*), had a notorious reputation for being naughty, brash, irreverent and very funny.

Up for a commercial, despite his many credits, Davey was asked for his picture and resume. Davey unzipped his fly, pulled out his penis and said, "Here, take a picture of this, it has a lot of resume."

John Raitt

With leading role credits like *Oklahoma, Carousel,* and *Annie Get Your Gun,* John was asked to read for the lead in the 1954 musical *Pajama Game,* involving labor problems in a factory. The part was Sid Sorokin, the plant superintendent with that great number "Hey There!"

John auditioned and was turned down by the one and only George Abbott, the director and co-author of the book with Richard Bissell, because Abbott thought John was "too square and un-hip" for the role.

Months later, after seeing almost everyone for the part, looking for the "right" Sid, Abbott called John and told him the part was his. Indeed it was. He was a hit in the show, and

Pajama Game was a huge success on stage and in the film with Doris Day.

B. S. Pully

Actor/comedian Pully had a varied career, in movie musicals for Fox in the '40s, and as a nightclub comic with a reputation of being outrageous with his highly offensive material. His deep and raspy bullfrog-like voice was unique. It was street all the way.

George S. Kaufman was directing the original stage musical *Guys and Dolls* on Broadway and was seeing people who looked and sounded like real New York types. Pully came to the auditions just to schmooze with one of his pals auditioning. As soon as he croaked, "Hello, pal," to his buddy, Kaufman snapped to attention.

Kaufman approached Pully and asked him could he handle a role where he'd have to play dice. Pully took out a pair of dice from his pocket and said, "You're faded." Pully got the role of Big Jule.

Anonymous

One casting director recalls "a very talented actor who came in, took out an orange, and proceeded to peel that orange and eat it while we talked. He was doing that to get attention, and you could say that he succeeded because I remember it, but I don't remember it with a good feeling. If anything, I found it to be pretentious."

Chapter Eight

If Only

Julia Roberts

Like many Hollywood scripts, *Pretty Woman* went through many hands, many writers, and transformations. Originally a dark script entitled *$3,000*—about Vivian Ward, a drug-addicted prostitute who is turned into Cinderella for a week by Edward Lewis, a wealthy businessman, then is sent back to the streets—it was bought by Disney and transformed into a fairy tale with the requisite happy ending.

Garry Marshall, one of the most sought-after directors in Hollywood, thought Julia would be a terrific Vivian. A meeting was set up with Touchstone (Disney). Casting Julia raised doubts. Could she handle a starring role in a big budget picture?

Marshall insisted she be tested. He thought she tested well but he "couldn't find where her funny bone was." He decided to test her against men: Tom Conti, Sam Neill, then Charles Grodin.

Marshall told Julia, "He's going to blow you off the screen." Grodin was hysterical, ad-libbing, when midscene Julia began to hold her own with him. He found her funny bone.

Marshall then told Disney even if they hadn't gotten their leading man yet, Julia could carry the picture. But Disney would not commit until Julia's agent, Elaine Goldsmith, told them Julia would take another movie if they didn't decide.

They finally agreed and signed Julia for three times what she had been paid for *Steel Magnolias*.

James Gandolfini

On Bravo's *Inside the Actor's Studio*, Gandolfini tells how he got to play the lead in HBO's huge hit *The Sopranos*.

"When I got the script and read it, I started to laugh out loud. There's no way I would get this part . . . they'll pick someone different than me . . . a suave good-looking mafioso type, more like a leading man.

"I went to the audition and halfway through it I stopped and said, 'This is not right, I'm not doing this right. I want to come back and read again.' They said 'OK.'

"I went back again and read again and got it. I realized . . . you've got to do it for yourself . . . not just to please them."

Elia Kazan

Several years ago, working late on a *Columbo* episode with Peter Falk in Los Angeles, I (Louis Zorich) got back to my hotel to find I had a couple of messages. The first was "Please call Elia Kazan in New York." I figured someone was putting me on. The second call was from my wife in New Jersey, "Call Elia Kazan." OK. No joke. It was real. But why me? I only met Kazan—or "Gadge," as he was called—once, and very briefly. So he really didn't know me.

Three days later, I was talking to Kazan in his home in New York about a sequel or prequel to his film *America, America*, and it was called *Beyond the Aegean*. We talked about the part of a Greek priest, and since I had a full white beard and moustache I looked like the Greek archbishop. After some general conversation with a cup of coffee and cookies, he handed me the script. I asked when could I come in and read for him. He shook his head and said, "You don't have to read, the part is yours."

The film never happened . . . he couldn't raise the money, but I'll never forget that Elia Kazan hired me without a reading, without bringing me back four times, without looking at my reel and without auditioning before ten or twelve people.

Laurence Fishburne

In the movie *King of New York*, Laurence had been slated to play the role of the policeman . . . but Laurence had other plans. Though the director, Abel Ferrara, had originally conceived the part of Jimmy Jump for a white actor, Laurence went to him and said, "I have an idea how the character, Jimmy, could be played. . . . Give me twenty-four hours, I'll come in and do it. If you don't like it, cool. I'll do the part that you want me to do."

Three days later, in the presence of the director, Abel, and the film's star, Christopher Walken, Laurence arrived in all of Jimmy Jump's iconic hip-hop flash: bowler, chain, gold tooth. For three hours, he told stories in character, playing his version of Jimmy, who "loved the fact that he was fast . . . loose, he could kill people." He won them over. He was Jimmy Jump.

Later, Laurence was quoted as saying it was the first time that anyone had given him "something to run with."

Jack Gilford

Auditions were being held for the Broadway musical *A Funny Thing Happened on the Way to the Forum*, with a score by Stephen Sondheim. Jack, a veteran of many shows, auditioned for the part of Hysterium twice and was turned down each time. Zero Mostel, who was signed to play the comic lead, was a friend of Jack's, and felt very strongly that Jack would bring a wonderful zany quality to the show, and he wanted Hal Prince and George Abbott and the creative people to see Jack at his best. He offered to read with Jack.

Zero and Jack rehearsed for several hours together before the audition, and Jack got the part with Zero's help. One of the writers, Larry Gelbart, said it was a generous act . . . "relatively unheard of, for stars rarely treat actors auditioning for supporting roles with such courtesy."

Billy Crystal

The name of Catch a Rising Star, a New York comedy club, truly proved prophetic. From four years of ensemble improv work to a solo act was a big leap for Billy, but he wanted it. Needing validation, he opened in a club and invited the man behind Woody Allen's rise, Jack Rollins. After the show Billy felt great. The audience loved him. Hoping to hear the same from Rollins, he sat down with him and listened. To his surprise Rollins, though he complimented Billy on getting his laughs, said Billy was playing it too safe . . . he wasn't daring enough, but worse, he didn't see Billy in the work, he wasn't personal enough. Billy took his advice, worked on being who he uniquely was and according to Billy . . . that's when he became a comedian.

Billy did his twenty-five minutes . . . to a cheering crowd and Jack. After, in a coffee shop, Billy, fully expecting Jack to say, "I'm dumping Woody . . . you're my guy . . . nobody else," . . . was shocked and surprised to hear Jack say, "You got big laughs, your impressions were wonderful . . . but never once did I hear you say how *you* felt about anything . . . you didn't take risks . . . you're playing it too safe . . . don't be afraid to bomb."

"That's when I began to get personal in my work . . . to take chances. That's when I became a comedian," Billy said.

Dame Edith Evans

William Gaskill, the eminent British director, wanted very much to see the legendary British actress Dame Edith about playing Queen Margaret in Shakespeare's *Richard III*. When Dame Edith arrived she sat down with Gaskill and they went through her text . . . line by line. When she was convinced that they agreed on an approach, she accepted the part. Not before.

Saul Rubinek

Rubinek tells this story:

In 1968 in Toronto the only theatre where you could get paid real money at that time was something called Theatre Toronto, run by Clifford Williams. I arranged to try out for an apprentice position, which meant I would probably carry a spear.

My standard audition pieces were a medieval piece, Bosola from *The Duchess of Malfi*, and a Renaissance piece, Malvolio's letter scene from *Twelfth Night*, both of which are lengthy. In the middle of the audition, I began to realise that it was not going well. I was boring. It was awful. Clifford Williams and a couple of others were barely looking up. I knew I was dying in this audition but somehow I had to save face. I had somehow to come out of this with some dignity intact, so I stopped abruptly in midsentence.

"What did you say your season was?"

Boy, did heads look up. Suddenly everyone was looking at me. Finally I've got them. I repeated the question. They were completely thrown. "Well, we're doing *The Deputy* and . . ." they continue to list their season. I listened, nodding.

"Nah, I'm not really interested." And I left.

Arthur Penn

Penn, director in both theatre and film, was auditioning actresses for the female lead in William Gibson's two-character play *Two for the Seesaw*. He, Gibson, and the play's producers saw many actresses for the very open, spontaneous and earthy part of Gittel Mosca, but they felt no one was really right until an actress named Anne Bancroft came out on stage, looked out at them, and asked, "Where's the john?"

This was all they needed. They had their Gittel Mosca.

Chris Cooper

Chris, after his outstanding work in films like *The Patriot* and *American Beauty*, clearly had a lot going for him when he went in to audition for Spike Jonze, the director of *Adaptation*.

Chris, in reading each scene of the character John LaRoche, gave or offered Jonze four or five different interpretations.

Jonze's enthusiasm, mutual trust, and respect gave Chris the freedom and license to audition so imaginatively that the two agreed on using this approach during the shooting of the film.

It was this film, *Adaptation*, that won the Oscar for Chris Cooper as Best Supporting Actor.

Erich Von Stroheim

Hollywood, 1926. Von Stroheim was casting what was going to be the most extravagant of all Von Stroheim productions, *The Wedding March*. One matter held up the production: he had no Mitzi, the young leading lady. After a troublesome experience with Mae Murray, he was determined not to engage a well-known star. The search was on. He reviewed all actresses under contract at Paramount. Then one day a talent scout, Mrs. Schley, brought in nineteen-year-old girl,

Fay Wray, just out of high school with a few minor screen credits. Miss Wray recalls:

"The office was rather dark. Von Stroheim sat behind his desk and in a corner sat his secretary. He didn't talk to me at all, but I knew he was watching me as he chatted with Mrs. Schley. Presently he said, looking at me at last: 'Are you sure you can do the part?'

"'I know I can,' I replied, but I was all a-tremble.

"Then he swung about in his swivel chair.

"'Whom does she look like to you, Mrs. Westland?' he asked.

"'Mitzi,' answered his secretary. Not a word more. That was all.

"Then Von Stroheim rose and approached me. He put his hand over mine: 'Goodbye, Mitzi.'

"I broke into tears. I couldn't help it. The part was right for me. I knew I would get it when I read it. But when Von Stroheim said, 'Goodbye, Mitzi,' it was just too much.

"Mrs. Schley cried and Mrs. Westland cried and there were tears in Von Stroheim's eyes. They left me there, and I sat weeping in the dark."

Von Stroheim said, "As soon as I saw Miss Wray and spoke to her, I knew I had the right girl. I didn't even test her. . . . I select my players from a feeling that comes to me when I am with them, a certain sympathy or vibration that exists between us that convinces me that they are right. I could not work with a girl who did not have a spiritual quality. . . . Fay had it and a very real sex appeal that takes hold of the hearts of men."

Michael J. Fox

Family Ties, a TV sitcom, saw Michael for the role of Alex Keaton and rejected him outright. Well, the head of the network, Brandon Tartikoff, did. His reason? Michael was way too short, in fact he was small, while his TV parents would not be. Simply unacceptable. Then along came Gary David Goldberg, the producer of the show and fervent champion of Michael.

"This guy is amazing. You send him out to get two laughs, he comes back with five."

That convinced Brandon, but he had to say that "this is not the kind of face you'll ever see on a lunch box." Of course the show was very successful. And one day a lunch box was received by Brandon, and a face on it was Michael J. Fox.

Oh, yes, a note inside said, "Eat crow, Tartikoff."

Nehemiah Persoff

Persoff shares this story:

I was sent up to a posh New York hotel to meet with the director Otto Preminger, who was casting the film *The Man with the Golden Arm* starring Frank Sinatra. I arrived on time, waited for a half hour after my scheduled time, then lost my patience.

I told the secretary I couldn't wait any longer. She called Otto, who opened the door, through which I saw this buxom lady. "Please be patient, this is a very important meeting I'm having. Go into the next room, have a drink, make yourself comfortable, and I'll see you very shortly."

I walked into this luxurious room. Otto, obviously, was on an expense account. I had a scotch, picked up the newspaper, had three or four more drinks, got sleepy and went to sleep on his bed. Eventually, he woke me up. "Ok, I want you to read."

"Why do you want to read me, I've played this part many times. Have you seen *Al Capone, The Untouchables, Hawaii 5-0*?"

"Yes, I have," said Otto, "but I want to hear how you interpret this role."

"Otto, for that you'll have to pay my salary," said Persoff as he stumbled out of the hotel room . . . and, of course, the movie.

F. Murray Abraham

Abraham tells this story:

Up for a part in a play, *The Man in the Glass Booth*, directed by Harold Pinter, I was asked by Mr. Pinter to pantomime a tailor taking measurements . . . this after I had said to him, "You want to see some Shakespeare?" "We're not *doing* Shakespeare!"

At the end of the mime, he said, "Thank you." I said, "Is that it?" Mr. Pinter said, "I think we've seen what you can do."

"Do?! Do?! I don't think I've done *a goddamn thing!!!*" I said thank you, left the stage, and cried my little eyes out.

The next day he gave me the part—seventy-three words, I still remember.

Gemma Jones

Gemma, the very popular British actress, said that when she went into audition she had the attitude . . . do I want to work with this person?

Ed Asner

Grant Tinker, TV producer and husband of Mary Tyler Moore at the time, saw Asner playing a police chief in a movie, liked him, and brought him in to read for the part of Mary's boss on *The Mary Tyler Moore Show*.

Asner would later say, "I'd always been capable of doing comedy, but was always afraid of it because I didn't know how to do it and repeat it."

He read for them and they said, "Well, that was an intelligent reading," which meant it wasn't funny. Then they said, "When we have you back to read with Mary, we want you to read it wild, wiggy, funny . . . you know, far out."

According to Asner, "I didn't know what the hell they meant, so I started to walk out and I said, 'Let me try it that way now and if I can't do it, don't have me back.' So I read it like a meshuggener—like a crazy guy—and they laughed their asses off.

"They had me back to read with Mary, and I read it crazily again, got laughs and went out the door."

Mary looked at them and said, "Are you sure?"

"That's your Lou."

Humphrey Bogart

For Robert Sherwood's Broadway-bound play *The Petrified Forest*, director Arthur Hopkins was auditioning actors for the part of the killer, Duke Mantee. Hopkins felt Bogart's snarling reading wasn't what he was looking for, but the star, Leslie Howard, insisted Bogart *was* Duke Mantee. The play with Bogart was a big hit, so big that Warner Brothers signed him and Howard for the movie. In Hollywood, Bogart got the shock of his life when the studio made a switch, deciding to pay him off and use Edward G. Robinson instead. Furious, Bogart wired Howard, who issued an ultimatum: "It's either with Bogart or without me." The studio capitulated. Howard's immense favor wasn't forgotten. One of Bogart's daughters was named Leslie.

Charles Kimbrough

Responding to a request for an audition story, Charles, in *Murphy Brown* at the time, wrote: "I've been racking my brain trying to think of embarrassing stories . . . or even memorable ones . . . and I've come to the conclusion that they're either all excruciating or I'm in permanent, cheerful denial of reality. If it is the latter, I choose to stay that way!"

Bea Lillie

It was a very rough beginning for Bea. She was young, unemployed, and clueless on how to find work or wear proper clothes that would get her some attention. (A fellow actress suggested that a little lower neckline might be helpful.) One time Bea had three auditions on the same day. With the help of her mother, Bea found a suitable dress to wear, and off she went. At Bea's first audition, she demurely said to the producer, "I should like to sing 'Oh, for the Wings of a Dove.'" He listened politely and said, "Thank you."

At the next audition, Bea began singing "I Hear You Calling Me," but she was cut off after only a few bars with an unsympathetic "Thank you."

Her Irish rising, she thought, "I'll show them this time." Bea trudged to the third and last audition. Waiting her turn, Bea finally heard 'Next!' She daintily stepped out on stage and took a dramatic pause, bowed, and said, "Thank you," and made her exit.

Charles Grodin

Let Grodin tell the story his way:

I was being considered for the role in *Midnight Run*. I spent several hours on several days auditioning with Robert De Niro for the director. It couldn't have gone better, and yet after it was all over, the director called me from an airplane to arrange another audition. I asked what he would like to see that he hadn't seen. It was something about "more something." The static on the line prevented my hearing what he said.

Finally I told my agent, as a strategic move, that before I flew to Los Angeles to audition again, "Let's make sure we can make a deal," and then ask for more money than they intended to pay.

The director called back and said, "Would you take less if we forget about more auditions?" I said "yes," and we quickly made a deal.

Sean Rice / Mike Nichols

Sean Rice tells this story:

One New York City night in 1974 my phone rings.

"Is this Sean?"

"Yeah."

"This is Mike Nichols. I received your letter. You didn't include your phone number so I got it from SAG. I'm going over and over in my head trying to figure it out who you are. I'm curious to know exactly what part it is that I offered to you."

[Sean, stunned in silence, said,] "It was just to get your attention."

Silence.

Then he starts laughing, "That's terrific, I don't believe it. You got me. I just finished *The Fortune* two months ago. After this I'm sorry that there isn't anything I can offer you. You certainly got my attention that's for sure. I just couldn't imagine . . ." he's laughing away, "that I offered you . . . knowing the hardships of the business I can appreciate your trying your own way of getting ahead. Whatever it takes to get in the door. Bravo. Do send me a photo and resume. Perhaps one day."

Here's what Sean had written:

"Dear Mike: Hope you are well. I'm sorry to say I can't accept your offer, but I do wish you well with your project. All the best, Sean.

"P. S. Ann and Mel wish you well."

Helen Hunt

Helen shares this story:

"I fought very hard to get *As Good as It Gets*, but the director, James Brooks, said, 'No . . . she's too young.' Still he agreed to see me. I was so nervous because I loved his work and I wanted the part so badly. I hate wanting something so badly because then there's so much to lose. I read . . . and there was a guy with a video camera having me do it again and again. Then I came back and met Jack Nicholson so we'd have a sense of working together.

"After, Jim Brooks sat me down and said . . . 'I'm scared to do this, I'm scared about the age thing . . . I want you to do this part.' I said, you know what? You're not sure and you need to be sure, take a little time and be sure you want me.

"He later called me at home and said, 'I want you to play this part'" . . . .the part that got Helen the Oscar.

Tony Randall

An old theatre friend of mine from Chicago, Vernon Schwartz, gave me this wonderful story. He was involved with *The Odd Couple* in Chicago, starring Tony with a great cast of local actors: Tony Mockus, Joe Greco, Dick Sasso, and so on. A TV network man from New York, planning an *Odd Couple* series for the upcoming season, flew in to see the production and Tony playing Felix. He was very impressed with the show and Tony got the part.

Tony was so happy with the cast that he insisted that they all be flown to New York to audition. The TV executives already had in mind who they wanted, including Jack Klugman to play Oscar. The cast, though disappointed at the outcome, were highly pleased that Tony not only had such a high regard for them, but that he showed extraordinary generosity.

Henry Fonda

Fonda, in the early thirties, was appearing in a play, *The Swan*. Fonda met an actress, June Walker, whose husband Geoffrey Kerr shared Fonda's dressing room. June had a new play by Marc Connelly called *The Farmer Takes a Wife*. Connelly was looking for an actor to play the leading role. June felt Fonda was ideal for the part and told Fonda she would arrange it for Connelly to see Fonda in the play. After the final curtain he invited Fonda to read for the title role in his suite at the Gotham Hotel in New York.

The next day, Connelly, a habitual late riser, greeted Fonda in his pajamas and directed him to the den. In Fonda's own words: "Marc wrote stage directions in between dialogue . . . it was literature. And he wanted me to appreciate it. So he waved me to a couch. Script in hand, and started to reading it to me.

"He began to play all the other characters. He was absolutely spellbinding. He read the whole damn play to me, he plopped himself on the couch. 'How was I?' and I told him the truth. 'Great! You've got the part,' said Connelly as his face lit up."

Sam Coppola

Sam gets an audition to read for Harold Becker, the writer and director of the movie *City Hall*, starring Al Pacino. His agent tells him to bring his tape with him.

The scene goes very well, but the vibes in the room tell Sam he doesn't stand a chance. Yet Mr. Becker compliments him effusively, saying, "You're a great actor!"

Sam, trusting his feelings, says, "Do you want to see my tape?"

(Long pause.) "Uh, well, yeah . . . sure . . . okay," Mr. Becker says, recovering.

Sam hands over his tape. "That will be three dollars."

Mr. Becker, a bit taken aback, pays Sam the three dollars. Sam was not in *City Hall*.

Jack MacGowran

Jack, the Irish actor who became a great exponent of Samuel Beckett's works, was short of money for a time in New York. An agent suggested he look for work in commercials since he had a deep, powerful voice with a hint of his native Dublin in it, which added to his charm.

Jack was sent up for a voice-over commercial that involved a Martian character. He read the copy superbly . . . only to be told that was not the way Martians talked. A stunned MacGowran asked politely, "How is it you know what a bloody Martian sounds like?"

No response was forthcoming. Jack stalked out and never attempted a commercial again.

Peter Sellers

Peter, very, very early in his career, went to audition for Hedley Claxton, an impresario who was casting his summer season revue for the Lido Theatre in Cliftonville, Margate. Sellers's routine was a patter, pretending to be that of an Indian journalist sending home his opinions of London to the *Pawnee Graphic*. It was a bit saucy.

He lost out to Benny Hill, who sang a calypso, accompanying himself on a guitar. After the audition, he bought Sellers coffee and cake at a local café, where they exchanged addresses and phone numbers and promised to pass on news of any jobs.

Benny, who worked on radio with Peter a few years later when Sellers was a big radio star, but his face was unknown, told *Picturegoer* to "watch Peter Sellers. He's going to be the biggest funnyman in Britain."

Max Weinberg

Max started playing the drums at the age of five. Years later, he played in the Broadway musical *Godspell* while attending Seton Hall University in New Jersey *and* playing in a club date band. Max was a busy drummer and life was pretty good.

One rehearsal day with his group, several members mentioned that they were auditioning for some unknown guy who had recorded for Columbia Records. Max was very upset at this, because he felt that together they had something good going and yet here they were auditioning for this guy nobody ever heard of, until one of the keyboard players said this guy was also auditioning drummers . . . and why doesn't Max check it out. Max thought if they were all auditioning, maybe he should. He did . . . and that's how he ended up with the E Street Band and that unknown guy, Bruce Springsteen.

Mickey Rourke

After appearing and starring in some thirty films, Mickey was cast as a villain in the movie *Picture Claire* with Gina Gershon. Mickey got the part after answering a casting call. They were looking for a "Mickey Rourke type."

Elizabeth Ashley

Elizabeth, a thirty-year-old actress and Broadway Tony and Drama Critics Award winner along with lots of TV credits, went to read for a small part in a movie in L.A. She walked into the office, where a dozen other actresses were waiting to audition.

The secretary looked up from reading *Cosmopolitan*, handed Elizabeth a script, and said, "Here, read this, they'll call you when they are ready." This was unusual for Elizabeth, but she needed the job.

Her turn came. The producer checked her up and down, then said, "Oh, yeah, didn't you used to do stuff a long time ago? Weren't you in some series or something?"

That really got to Elizabeth. She couldn't help herself. She rolled up the script and shoved it back at him.

"Do I have to tell you what to do with it? If you want my credits, look in *Who's Who in the American Theatre*!"

Liam Neeson

Casting in London for the film *The Empire of the Sun*, Steven Spielberg's people hired Neeson to read with the young actors who were auditioning for the lead, Jim. Neeson himself was not auditioning. When the casting was over, Spielberg was so impressed with Neeson's voice and presence that he said to Neeson, "We're going to do something special some day."

Three years later while in New York, Spielberg saw Neeson in the play *Anna Christie*, went backstage with Kate Capshaw, whose mom was so moved by Neeson that she wept. Neeson was so touched by her response that he embraced her. Capshaw later told Spielberg that that's exactly what Schindler would have done.

After a screen test, Neeson ended up doing that "something special" with Steven Spielberg . . . Oskar Schindler, in *Schindler's List*.

Joan Rivers

Joan auditioned for Second City in Chicago after waiting half a day in an outer office. She remembers being escorted to a conference room where Bernie Sahlins, the producer, and Paul Sills, the director, sat in judgment. According to Joan, "The phone rang and Sahlins took the call while I stood there like an idiot."

Paul Sills said, 'Improvise something.'

Joan asked for a script. Sills said, "We don't work with scripts. Just describe something—anything—whatever you think is happening in this room."

She exploded. "In this room is a cheap ugly little man sitting behind the telephone without the manners to get off and watch somebody who has been waiting five hours. And the other man, so superior, is saying, 'We don't have scripts.'"

She waxed eloquent and chucked an ashtray across the room. Then they talked, and the following day she was offered the job.

Joe Pesci

Casting for the movie *Raging Bull*, the story about the troubled boxer Jake La Motta, star Robert De Niro and director Martin Scorsese were looking for an actor to play Jake's brother. De Niro saw Pesci in a film, *The Debt Collector*, and found him really interesting. De Niro and Scorsese met with him.

Pesci, at this point, had decided to stop his acting career. His attitude was, "I don't need this, I don't need this from you or from anybody." So they sat down with him and said, "All right, no big deal, we'll talk and see if we can come to terms of any kind . . . or even if you want to read."

Pesci said, "I don't want to read for anybody." They agreed and they listened to him and talked, and they liked the way he spoke. He had a wonderful way of improvisation.

Pesci would later say, "I was worn out trying to be an actor. I had given up. I didn't want to get involved with acting again because I don't like the business of acting. I like acting as an art. I was a child actor on stage at four. My first film was *The Debt Collector* [1975].

"I was out of place in Hollywood, where you're at everybody's mercy all the time . . . you get to the point out there where you bump into walls and say, "Excuse me," so as not to offend anybody so you can get a job. I wanted to get away from all that and get back into the position where everybody treated you like a man. But when I met Marty and Bob I saw that working with them would be different."

Geoffrey Rush

Geoffrey talks about the film *Shine*, for which he won an Oscar:

"The script literally dropped out of heaven in 1992, although it wasn't filmed until 1995 for funding hiccups. My career had been in the theatre for twenty-three years with spits and coughs in bits and pieces in films."

Going up for the lead role, the director, Scott Hicks, said he didn't have to read . . . his entire career was his audition.

Robert Evans

Evans's early acting career was going nowhere. At nineteen he turned to modeling men's clothes and eventually represented a line of clothes on the west coast. Still with dreams of making it, and with the help of an agent, he auditioned and was signed by Paramount Pictures. He went through a rigorous training period, but after six months Paramount dropped their option on him. He went back to New York to work with his brother's firm, Evan-Picone, where he soon became a fashion celebrity traveling all over the United States.

In L.A., Evans stayed at the posh Beverly Hills Hotel, where he had a suite and cabana by the pool and a telephone, which he used constantly. Nearby on chaise lounges were Marty Arrouge and his wife, the Hollywood icon Norma Shearer. "Are you an actor . . . why are you always on the phone?" Norma and her husband had been watching Evans by the pool for a couple of days, admiring his presence and authority . . . "He's perfect, he's Irving," said Norma to her husband.

She asked Evans, "Would you like to play my husband?" She was referring to the part of Irving Thalberg, her late husband, in the film *The Man with a Thousand Faces* with James Cagney. Shearer had casting approval.

That's how Robert Evans became the "boy wonder" boss at Universal Studios . . . playing Irving Thalberg. Ironically, years later, Robert Evans became the *real* "boy wonder" head of Paramount Pictures . . . the very studio that, earlier in his career as an actor, had dumped him.

Monica Parker

Parker shares this story:

I auditioned for Alan Parker (*Evita, Fame, Midnight Express*), who is not in fact a relation, for the strangest script I had ever read. It was called *The Road to Wellville.* I auditioned once, I auditioned twice, three, four times. It was always exactly the same, always on tape. I wore the same outfit, hair the same way, everything.

I started to wonder if this was some kind of perverse fetish for him, because he had never asked me to do anything different. Finally I said, "Alan, your last name is Parker. Somewhere we're related. I've waited my whole life for nepotism. Just give me the job."

And he did.

Richard Russell Ramos

In L.A., Richard was simply not getting any auditions as an actor. Nothing. Determined to find out why, he went to see his agent.

Agent: "Did you see your pictures? They're horrible . . . who would hire you? Get new pictures."

Richard: "Is it because of my pictures?"

Agent: "Not only your pictures."

Richard: "What is it then?"

Agent: "The casting people."

Richard: "What is it?"

Agent: "They hate you. The last audition you did was awful. They don't like you."

Richard (beginning to get angry): "None of them? What about my talent?"

Agent: "What about it?"

Richard: "I've been an actor for twenty years, theatre, TV, films. I'm a good working actor and you say they *hate* me???!!"

Agent: "Well, what can I tell you?"

Richard: "You're my agent, what do you think?"

Agent (pause): "Truthfully, I never liked you either."

Richard (now in a rage): "Well, go fuck yourself!!!"

Richard storms out of the office out to the parking lot, sees his agent's car there . . . lets the air out of all four tires and walks away.

Roscoe Lee Browne

Roscoe, a one-time athlete and instructor, and at the time employed at a public relations firm, decided to change his life. At thirty-five, he wanted to go into theatre. Three of his friends who were in theatre—Josephine Premice, Susan Fonda, and Leontyne Price—were shocked that he would want to leave a well-paying, secure position in the business world to try to become an actor in the wildly unpredictable world of theatre, particularly being black and thirty-five years old. Ms. Price felt he'd be lucky to work as an extra.

Roscoe, checking the trade papers, saw that Joe Papp's Shakespeare Theatre was holding auditions. Somehow he got in to read for Stuart Vaughn and Joe, who asked him how long he had been an actor. Roscoe said, "Twelve hours . . . and I don't want to be a spear carrier."

Joe laughed and promised him he'd get parts, which he did in eight different Shakespeare plays. Roscoe recalls with gratitude and affection what it meant for Joe Papp to hire him with absolutely no theatrical experience *and* at the age of thirty-five: "He changed my life."

George Lucas

According to Walter Beakel, who worked for many years in Hollywood as a director, talent agent, and teacher, Lucas (*Star Wars*, *The Empire Strikes Back*) did not ask for acting credits when casting. He trusted his feeling for the person in front of him, the human being. To Walter's knowledge, producer/director Lucas never auditioned anyone.

Bob Hoskins

True story as told to Dustin Hoffman by Bob himself:

It may not be a hundred percent accurate, but it's as close to it as I remember it. Bob (*In America*, *A Truck*) was a London lorry driver, and one day he stopped off at a pub for a drink or two. He was "half-in-the-bag" when he felt a tap on his shoulder. Turning, he was told, "Your turn to read." Bob, reflexively, said, "Buy me a drink."

Before he knew it, he was in a room with four people sitting in an empty chair. For a moment he thought they were perverts. "Half-in-the-bag" Bob found himself in the empty chair with some papers. "You can read now," he was told. Bob read . . . to himself, clueless as to what was going on. Some comments were passed and Bob said, "Oh, but if you want me to read *aloud* it'll cost you another drink." Here the details get hazy, but Bob apparently showed them enough to warrant another drink and another go at it.

Bob got the part in the play in one of those pub theatres in and around London, and years later he was an excellent

Iago to Anthony Hopkins's Othello. Not bad for an ex-lorry driver!

Willem Dafoe

With the Theatre X Company appearing at a festival in Baltimore, Willem bumped into performance group founder Richard Schechner at the adjoining urinal. Schechner, at one point, turned to him and said, "You have a look, you'd be very good in my play."

Willem became a member of the New York–based performance group.

Bill Hinnant

Bill was up for a dog food commercial, auditioning in the client's office.

Client: "We want you to get down on all fours, like a dog, and go up to this bowl of dog food and eat it."

Bill: "You want me to . . ."

Client: "Yeah, you'll be in a dog suit and you go eat the dog food."

Bill: "So . . . on the set . . . I'll be in a dog suit and do it."

Client: "Yeah . . . but we want to see *how* you do it."

Bill: "Without the suit?"

Client: "Yeah, here's the dog food."

The client takes an ashtray full of butts and ashes and places it on the floor.

Bill: "You want me to crawl on the floor and show you how I'd eat it."

Client: "Now you got it."

Bill picked up the ashtray and dumped it on the client's desk.

Bill: "Now *you* got it."

Burl Ives

How did Burl get the part of Big Daddy, the dying Southern patriarch, in the original production of Tennessee Williams's *Cat on a Hot Tin Roof?* The usual way, you know, auditioning.

"I got into a brawl in a saloon in Greenwich Village. Elia Kazan, the director, happened to be there and saw me throw out some hecklers and figured there was some of Big Daddy in me."

John Corbett

According to Nia Vardalos, star and writer of her hugely successful romantic comedy of 2002, *My Big Fat Greek Wedding,* she was in a Los Angeles bar with one of the film's producers trying to decide on a male lead, with John Corbett of *Sex and the City* in mind, when Corbett suddenly walked into the bar.

They had found their male lead.

Albert Brooks

Brooks, an actor, writer, and director, was raised mostly by his mother, Thelma Leeds. His father, Harry Einstein, was a radio comedian who died onstage during a Friar's Club roast in 1958.

Brooks co-wrote the movie *Mother* with collaborator Monica Johnson. Casting and auditioning for the part of the mother was not easy for Brooks. A decade earlier, he might have asked his own mother to play Beatrice, the mother, but now she was too old. He wanted to score a casting coup to play opposite someone who hadn't been seen onscreen in awhile. "There are two kinds of mothers in the world," said Brooks, "the one that approves of everything, and the other . . . this movie is about the other."

Nancy Reagan. One of Brooks's first stops was Nancy Reagan's house. After some readings, the former film actress

Nancy Davis told him, "This is going to kill me for the rest of my life, but I can't do this." Monica Johnson reasoned that if Reagan had died during the shooting, the movie's insurance policy wouldn't have covered the disruption caused by a state funeral.

But Brooks said, "Oh God, no, it was never that literal. Imagine Nancy Reagan's position. She's still one of the most famous people in America, a former first lady, and [Ronald Reagan's] still alive and hopefully well. It was just about her leaving his side." Scott Rudin, the producer, for one, was relieved. "I thought it was the kind of stunt that would be an interesting announcement and probably a bad movie."

Doris Day. Brooks went to see Doris, now an animal-rescue activist living in Carmel. "I've never seen so many dogs in my life," said Brooks, "their heads were in every window. They all started barking . . . twenty-six dogs barking at you . . . scary! They live three or four to a room; they have doggie beds."

Over lunch at her country club, Doris turned him down. "It was interesting," he says, "because I think she reached the decision in my presence that she didn't want to be in movies anymore."

Esther Williams. Brooks had seen her on a talk show acting "very motherly." He went to see her at her house. They rehearsed a seven-page scene in which Brooks's mother tries to serve him some ancient, crusted-over off-brand ice cream out of her freezer. "Esther acted very well; she made me laugh," Brooks said.

But he couldn't help noticing that inside her freezer was Häagen-Dazs. For him, this symbolized the basic difference between Williams and Beatrice, Brooks's mother in the movie. "I didn't want Esther to act a person that she wasn't," he says. "She's so upset—she told someone, 'If I didn't have Häagen-Dazs, I would've had the part.'"

Debbie Reynolds. Debbie hadn't acted since 1971, so Brooks called Carrie Fisher, her daughter, and asked, "Do you think she could play this part?"

With Carrie's urging and after seeing the script, Debbie read. After they read a scene, Brooks told her, "Well, that's fine."

"What's fine?" Debbie asked.

"Well, you have it, I'd love you to do it."

"Albert, you can't take me by one reading, ask me to read another scene."

"I don't have to," he said.

"Albert, I don't understand, is this how it's done today? You had me read one scene, and not the important one, and I got it?"

"Now you sound like my mother."

"Oh," Debbie said, "so I just did the other scene."

"That's right," Brooks said.

Kathleen Widdoes

Kathleen did her homework, really worked on the part, and was waiting to read for a movie to be directed by Jon Peters, who at one time was Barbra Streisand's hairdresser, then director, and then producer—and, at one point, along with Peter Guber, he ran Sony Studios. Kathleen waited for one hour; one hour turned to two. Mr. Peters finally arrived very, very late to see Kathleen, sat down, and said, "You have a hole in your blouse."

Kathleen, after more than a two-hour wait, said, "And you have a hole in your ass," got up and walked out.

Anonymous

And then there was this performer at a musical audition, who in the middle of his "up-tempo" number was abruptly told, "Thank you!"

He came back with "You're welcome!" And kept right on singing!

Juanita Hall

Director Josh Logan, in casting the Rodgers and Hammerstein musical *South Pacific*, had a relatively easy time getting the two leads, Mary Martin and Ezio Pinza. A tougher role to cast was Bloody Mary. But at an audition, Juanita Hall, a marvelous singer, took off her shoes and stockings and struck a squatting pose that said, "I am Bloody Mary and don't you dare cast anyone else!"

He didn't.

Deborah Kerr

In lining up the leads for his proposed filming of George Bernard Shaw's play *Major Barbara*, the producer, Gabriel Pascal, had Rex Harrison and Wendy Hiller but hadn't found the actress to play the young Salvation Army girl. Lunching with a friend at the Savoy in London, he described what he was looking for: "A pure, innocent girl with a spiritual face."

A few tables away were a girl and an older woman. Mr. Pascal spotted them. Something about the girl intrigued him. Without hesitation he went up to them and to the girl said, "Are you a virgin?" The girl was embarassed. Mr. Pascal, undeterred, said, "I think you can act." He offered to read her after lunch if she would "recite something for me."

The girl, a dancer with Sadler's Wells, went off with her friend to the ladies' room and returned prepared with a piece she knew. She barely opened her mouth when Mr.

Pascal asked her to say the Lord's Prayer. She did . . . and Mr. Pascal had tears in his eyes.

"You are the girl." The girl was Deborah Kerr.

Don Adams

Don (later to star in the TV series *Get Smart*), as an up-and-coming performer in New York, came up with a really unique way to audition. Garry Moore was seeing him for his show.

"Mr. Moore," he began on the studio stage, "Don Adams is not really my name. My father was a famous star in the theatre. I don't want to trade on his name . . . but if I were to tell you, a tear would come to your eye, there'd be a lump in your throat. You know him . . . I know you loved him. . . . Oh, well, I might as well tell you his name. . . ."

Long pause; Adams's face went blank. "Funny, I was just talking to him the other day. His name is. . . ." He began searching inside his jacket pocket. "I know I had it here somewhere . . . it's. . . ."

"Thank you, Mr. Adams, that's all we need," Garry Moore said over the intercom.

Adams looked destroyed, "But Mr. Moore, you haven't heard my act yet."

"We don't need to hear the rest," Moore replied, by this time in the studio, "with a start like that, it's got to be great."

Will Patton

Will, on his trip to Los Angeles:

Most of the people you're dealing with from L.A. and in the movies are talking on the phone while you're looking at them. They're a really horrible bunch of people.

Someone flew me out there one time for a TV thing, I walked into the room, they were talking, and I said, "What's going on in this room? What happened? Did you just have an argument, or what? There's something very strange going on here."

They looked at me like, "What do you mean? This is the way we are, this is the way we behave."

I went out to the outer office and said to this guy, "Get me on a plane right away or I'm going to hit somebody."

That was my experience in L.A.

Jennifer Darling

Jennifer, a diminutive actress, went to audition for director Otto Preminger, who was casting a movie. Preminger, notorious for his bluntness (some would say cruelty), was equally famous for the spaciousness of his office, the likes of which reportedly was somewhat the size of half of a football field, with his desk at the far reaches of the room. So when the actor entered, if he or she wasn't intimidated by the distance that had to be covered, then the room wasn't doing its job.

Jennifer took one step into the room, was about to take that long daunting walk . . . when Preminger bellowed, "You're too short!"

Whereupon Jennifer shot right back with "And you're *ugly*!" She turned around and left.

"O.K., the role you're auditioning for is a struggling actress who's always boring people with stories of how this one or that one got the part she deserved because she's younger or prettier. Think you can handle it?"

Chapter Nine

What!? And Leave Show Business?

John Travolta

Theatre was in John's blood, just as it was in his mother's, brothers', and sisters'. John wanted it all—singing, dancing, acting. He worked hard at it, and at the tender age of seventeen he auditioned in New York for the lead in the Broadway musical *Jesus Christ Superstar.* John came close but didn't get it. A summer stock revival of *The Boy Friend* came to his attention, and John went to try out with high hopes. After the audition, the ninety-three-year-old producer said, "There are people here who can sing and dance better than you. But nobody has as much fun on stage. I can't resist you. You're contagious. I am going to hire you because I have so much fun watching you."

Barbra Streisand

In the sixties, an ill-fated musical entitled *Bravo, Giovanni* was being put together starring Cesare Siepi, an opera singer, and Michelle Lee. It was directed by Stanley Prager. It had been decided that the understudy for Ms. Lee would probably play matinees due to the strenuous demands of the role. The physical requirements stressed a "certain earthy quality." Many singer/actresses prominent on Broadway auditioned for the role, including Ms. Streisand, who was appearing in a small role in *I Can Get It for You Wholesale* but stopping the show with a song, "Miss Marmelstein." It was a mystery why she would want to leave that situation for an understudy part in an untried production.

At any rate, she appeared, some forty minutes late, dressed as any typical flower-child of the period would be, and dragging her guitar and barstool. It had been chaotic that day, since the Broadhurst Theatre had been procured at the last minute, and when auditions began, the cleaning ladies in the balcony hadn't finished restoring the theatre from the previous evening's performance, so there was vacuuming, etc., going on.

Ms. Streisand came out and set her stool down front . . . when suddenly she ran into the wings and complained about the "visitors" in the balcony, but was assuaged when told who they were and to ignore them.

She came out again, sat on the stool and started to sing. Never has a hush fallen so quickly over a group out front. Even the cleaning ladies up in the balcony stopped what they were doing and stared down at the stage. Everyone was mesmerized. Then Barbra finished her number, picked up her stool, tucked her guitar under her arm and rocketed out of the stage door, leaving the stage managers completely agape.

Out front . . . silence. Then the director's voice broke the quiet: "Well, she may be earthy and she can certainly sing, but she sure is homely!"

Peter Finch / Sidney Lumet

For his movie *Network*, director Lumet was searching for the right actor for the key part of Howard Beale. Finch, the well-known British/Australian actor, wanted to be seen for the part of the American TV personality, but Lumet felt he wasn't right for it because of Finch's accent. Finch contacted Lumet and insisted he could play the part. He got the international edition of the *Herald Tribune* daily and read the paper aloud from front to back for weeks, then submitted the tape to Lumet. Lumet was not only convinced, but very impressed.

Finch got the part . . . and an Oscar.

Liev Schreiber

Eric Bogosian was Schreiber's first role model. He saw Eric at a place called Danceteria. "This nut job called Ricky D. doing a queer insane lounge act . . . growling and rolling through the crowd giving people shit, and they were throwing drinks and spitting on him. It was very punk rock, and I thought, 'Holy shit! Here it is! A new relationship to the audience.'" It was Eric Bogosian.

Schreiber began to perform some of Bogosian's angry monologues and wrote solo pieces of his own . . . "cheap rip-offs of Eric's." Even after Yale Drama School and London's Royal Academy, Schreiber felt Bogosian's pull. He tried out for Bogosian's *SubUrbia* in '94.

"I made the huge mistake of telling him that he was my idol. . . . I wasn't getting any further in the audition."

David Ackroyd

David shares these stories:

1. For some auditions, I had to "go to the network," a process comprising a series of steps certain to mortally wound the ego of any sane person. On the same day, at the same hour, all the candidates (four or five for each role) for all the parts in the pilot arrive at the network headquarters to audition one final time. Before any actor gets to read, however, he must look over and sign his contract, which has been negotiated previous to arriving at this step and could possibly rule the next seven years of his life. This sometimes produces

frantic phone calls to agents over some clause or amount of
money that sounds dubious to the actor.

Then everyone gets to sit around and size up the competition for a while. (These things never start closer than an
hour to the appointed time.) This is a particularly daunting
experience, especially if one or more of the competition is
a celebrity or an actor whose work you really admire. Then,
one at a time, you get to go in to fourteen or so suits whose
collective attitude is a combination of your unworthiness to
be in their presence and how improbable it is that anything
you can do will in any way impress them. The business is
done as quickly and efficiently and impersonally as a visit
to a brothel and then it's time for the next john (unless the
auditioner is a celebrity and then he/she is fawned over,
jokes are laughed at, and some ritual acknowledgement is
made of his/her reality as a human being).

2. I did not, however, have to "go to the network" for a certain TV movie. I was told that I was being considered for
a leading role opposite Sharon Gless—in fact, I had been
told that the part was all but mine. Then suddenly the producer, Virginia Palance, who had looked at quite a bit of
film on me, was having some unidentified second thoughts
and wanted to meet with me. It was a wonderful role that I
wanted quite badly, so I agreed to the meeting, although I
had no idea what I could do in person to win the role that I
had not done better on screen.

Ms. Palance was an elegant and still beautiful redhead
of "a certain age" and we chatted for awhile and although I
couldn't understand what her reservations were, I inferred
that it had something to do with the fact that the role was
that of an absolute "nice guy" and that Ms. Palance detected
in my acting, even when playing "nice guys," an edge, a hint
of danger that she wasn't sure was right for the role. I tried

my best to be charming and nice and explain that, to me, nobody is totally nice and characters who hinted at some sort of edge were far more interesting than bland leading men.

She seemed finally to agree with me somewhat reluctantly and as the meeting drew to an end, she studied me closely a long time and then said, "It's just that you remind me of my ex-husband." Then the penny dropped—although I still can't see it, something about my acting and presence (and I must say I'm flattered by it) reminded her of Jack Palance, a remembrance which was obviously not a pleasant one for her. I went home and phoned my agent to tell her to forget about this one.

To Ms. Palance's credit, I got the job.

3. I have, of course, had my share of absolute humiliations in the auditioning process, but perhaps the most perplexing was when Neil Simon, Manny Azenberg, and Gene Saks came to L.A. to cast the Broadway production of *Rumors*. Although the thought of auditioning for the late twentieth century's King of Comedy was somewhat intimidating, the play was funny, I had a line on the character I was reading for, and I had a history with Manny. I had taken over for John Rubenstein in Manny's Broadway production of *Children of a Lesser God*. We had gotten on quite well, I thought, and even flattered myself that he liked my performance. I thought the reading might even be fun, given the nature of the material and the fact that Manny could grease the wheels a little.

The auditions were being held in a church annex in Hollywood, and I got there somewhat early to let myself settle in and get relaxed before the reading. But they were running a little early, of all things, and I was next up when I arrived. Ken McMillan came out of the audition room looking particularly gloomy, but then I didn't know him and he often looked that way on screen. Now it was my turn.

The casting director said nothing as we walked down the hall and entered the room, which was enveloped in an ominous silence. The casting director said simply, "This is David Ackroyd." Mr. Simon, Mr. Saks, and Manny looked as glum as it is possible for three of the most successful men in the American theatre to look. Mr. Simon and Mr. Saks merely nodded vaguely in my direction. I greeted Manny as enthusiastically as possible given the rapidly fading state of my confidence, to which he replied something along the lines of "How are you?" and nothing more.

Need I say that my reading, which I thought was pretty good under the circumstances, was greeted with a silence reminiscent of that to "Springtime for Hitler." What I had thought would be an atmosphere of barely restrained hilarity turned out to be, in fact, like being in a room with Samuel Beckett, Sam Nunn, and Oliver Cromwell. Never have I seen three more dour faces, nor do I ever hope to. Actually, they did me a favor in a way. When I left the audition, I felt sorrier for them than I did for myself.

Bruce Willis

Willis's career almost didn't happen. After showing up for an audition with his head shaved and wearing combat fatigues, he was rejected eleven times by ABC executives for the part on *Moonlighting* that launched him as private detective David Addison, because they didn't think anyone would take him seriously as Benedict to Cybill Shepherd's Beatrice.

Finally, during yet another casting meeting, the sole female executive in the room stood up and said, according to Glenn Gordon Caron, the show's creator, "I don't know if he's a leading man or not, I don't know if he's a TV star or not, but guys, I gotta tell you, he sure looks like a dangerous fuck to me!"

That, in Caron's words, "completely sucked the air out of the room," and the rest, as they say, is history.

Tom Brennan

1. Tom, who has done everything one can do in theatre, arrives to audition for a new play being done at a well-respected theatre outside of New York City. Plays originating here have made successful transfers to Off-Broadway, so Tom felt the prospects of this particular show to move were quite good.

He walks into the lobby of the theatre and over to a table to sign in, when he sees a card on the table, which had printed on it these words: Name actors are wanted.

2. A young man comes on stage auditioning for the musical *Meet Me in St. Louis*. He hands the sheet music to the pianist, who begins to play as the young man unzips his fly and not only lets it all hang out, but waves it up and down, singing, "Ding, ding, ding went the trolley. . . ."

John Phillip Law

John Phillip Law tells this story:

Years ago I successfully played Charlton Heston's son, Noel Hoxworth, in the epic James Michener film *The Hawaiians*, produced by the Mirisch Company. Much later my agent sent me to audition for a television show guest-starring Charlton Heston, in which they were insistent that the actor have the stature and ability to hold his own with Chuck. Photos, resumes, and the required boilerplate were sent to the casting director, and I enthusiastically went for the meeting thinking that I had this one in the bag. Upon arriving I was kept waiting for about forty minutes, then was ushered into the office of a very young casting director, who was clutching all my material in her hands. I listened patiently for ten minutes while she reiterated all information I had already been told. Upon finishing her speech she looked me squarely in the eyes and asked me what I had done.

Bruce Turk

The following story is an indication of the lengths an actor will go to for a particular job.

Bruce Turk first saw the Suzuki Company, a theatre group from Japan, when they performed *The Trojan Women* at the Chicago International Theatre Festival. Though the performance was in Japanese and he didn't speak a word, Bruce was impressed by their power and intensity.

Two years later, he went to Tokyo. From there he went to Toga, a small town in the mountains, where the Suzuki Company was offering an intensive physical and vocal training course. The course used techniques that were influenced by Kabuki, Noh theatre, and Kendo, a form of martial arts. Bruce spent up to six hours a day stomping, walking on the sides of his feet, walking in a squatting position, singing in unusual positions and so on.

When the company returned to Tokyo, he followed. He went to their business office, asked what needed to be done, and for eight months stuffed envelopes and did other office chores. For no money. Since he wasn't being paid, he also worked as an English teacher and as a clown in Tsurumai Park.

During this time, he practiced his training with another aspiring actor, who was Japanese and was also working gratis in the company's office. When the company went back to Toga (a small town in the mountains), Bruce followed again, this time sleeping in a tent.

When they offered their course in Saratoga, New York, he flew to Saratoga and enrolled.

At the end of the course, Tadashi Suzuki, the founder and artistic director, asked Bruce to join the company.

He was the only member who was not Japanese.

Elliott Gould

After appearing in a number of movies and then turning down a starring role as Lenny Bruce on Broadway, refusing to star in Robert Altman's *McCabe and Mrs. Miller,* and saying no to Sam Peckinpah's *Straw Dogs,* Gould chose to work with the celebrated Swedish director Ingmar Bergman in *The Touch.*

Working with Bergman turned Gould inside out . . . his mind was messed up. He wound up fighting with everyone, his production company broke up, he walked off the set of a new movie and had to pay Warners a penalty. He didn't work for eighteen months.

Then along came *The Long Goodbye.* Before signing him to one-quarter of his pre-Ingmar rate, United Artists insisted that he take not just a physical but a sanity test.

Anonymous

According to one actress, "My strangest and worst audition was for a movie in London. I had met the director in Los Angeles, but when casting and auditioning time came, he flew me to London. I really worked on the part, I wanted the job so desperately . . . a dramatic role of a sexual killer, ripping off my top, simulating masturbation, etc. My audition was amazing. When I finished, the director tells me I was really great . . . but oops! . . . he thought I was someone else! He flew me to London because he mistook me for *another* actress!"

David Chandler

David shares this story:

A docudrama movie of the week. When I arrived the actors already there had been waiting for more than an hour. The parts are small. The dialogue is entirely expository. I greet each familiar face, chat, complain, joke, pace, study my creased sides, visit the men's room. Two hours later I am ushered into an airless office, where the owl-eyed casting agent and her blithering assistant sit like mummies. The director, a Brit with bad hair and even worse teeth, hangs up the phone and turns to me, all penitence, and apologizes effusively for keeping me waiting.

What am I to say? Is this how you run your set? Is this why you can't get work in England, you snaggle-toothed cluck?

Well, of course not. I cheerfully demur: no problem, no problem. I start to read my five pathetic lines with their insurance-policy cadences and stunning intellectual pith. He thanks me when I'm done and asks me to brush my hair back. My hair is very short. I don't have a brush. I mat it down as best I can. I read again.

He thanks me and gives me an adjustment—acting, not tonsorial. He wants less. I can do less. I read. I do less. He thanks me, asks me to read again. And do even less. I read. I do less. He thanks me and asks me to read again. He's excited now. He wants more of what I just did, in other words, he wants more of less. I try very hard to do even more of less, five or six times . . . or the least that I can give.

It was not enough. I did not get the job.

Tom Kelly

1. Tom, one-time Broadway stage manager, recalls a Lincoln Center audition that involved one wonderful actor, the late Leonard Frey. He had introduced Leonard to some new hot director du jour, and the director had asked the usual

"Tell me a little about yourself" question, to which Leonard replied, in a politely withering tone, "No, no, dear boy, tell *me* a little about *your*self."

2. Tom remembers with horror the immediate period after everyone went and got *est*ed and believed they could achieve anything if they believed in it hard enough . . . like singing on key. People would come and sing horrendously for eight to sixteen bars of music with great conviction and zombie smiles, and you knew that they had been *est*ed (est was a consciousness-raising movement popular in the sixties and seventies, founded by Werner Erhard, named Erhard Seminars Training, commonly known as est).

Richard Jenkins

Early in his career as an actor, Richard was looking for an agent. One meeting stands out in his mind. He gave his picture and resume to this agent who, when examining his credits, said, "Sorry, we can't handle you."

Richard, with his extensive credits, asked, "Why not?"

The agent pointed to a line on the resume, *School for Wives*. Richard replied, "Yes?"

"We don't do any 'porn' here."

Richard continued his search for an agent.

Elaine Stritch / Alan Willig

A casting person sends talent agent Willig a movie script for one of his more high-profile actresses, namely, Ms. Stritch, along with a cover letter raving about how wonderful the part was, etc., etc. Alan reads the script and is shocked, to say the least. The role to be considered is an old Jewish grandmother and is all of *five* lines. Deeply insulted, Alan calls the casting person: "How in God's name did you see my client as an old Jewish grandmother when she has the map of Ireland on her face? Furthermore, what you call 'the part' has only *five* lines!"

The casting person replied, "Yes, but the camera will be on her all the time."

Fred Coffin

Fred tells this story:

Norman Jewison and Al Pacino were auditioning actors for an important supporting role in the film *And Justice for All*. I was very prepared, totally focused, and it happened. Leaving, the casting director ran up to me and whispered, "If you don't hear from us by three o'clock on Monday, it's over. Count on it."

Two o'clock on Monday passed . . . I waited and waited, and at 3:15 I stood up and screamed, "FUCK IT!!!" I put on my sneakers and hit Riverside Park for a punishing five-mile run, returned to the apartment to shower and die. No messages, no calls, no job.

I am not now nor was I then a junky, but someone had left some cocaine lying about. But this day, this moment, I wanted to get away from the real world as much as possible. I snorted the coke, smoked a joint and had three fast beers. I was totally cooked.

Then the phone rang. The casting director: "Come now!" click.

Numb and panic-stricken, I let out a primal scream . . . "NOOOOOOOO!!!!!!"

I grabbed a cab. Gasping for air, trying not to freak out. I tried to decipher the words of the script. Completely inarticulate. At the audition, I babbled, stuttered, laughing hysterically, for no reason; I didn't know what was going on, what was being said, or who was saying it.

I only remember the look in Pacino's eyes when I left. There goes the "alien" . . . and there went the part.

Yusef Bulos

Bulos tells this story:

I'm auditioning for the musical *Promises, Promises*. Nervous, because I hadn't done that much singing, but nevertheless I was prepared. The director was this short stocky man, big white hair with several rings on each finger. He was neither polite nor welcoming. Somehow, I seemed to be intruding on him. I began my song, "I Like Him," from *The Man of La Mancha*, my one song from my one musical. As I sang, the director was looking at my resume and appeared to be impatient with me and my singing.

Then his poodle, also coiffed and bejewelled, came over and started to sniff my crotch *during* my song. I managed to get through one verse when the director muttered, "What is this?" while looking at my resume. . . . I stopped, walked over, and grabbed my picture from his hand and said, "This is ridiculous. At least you could give me some professional courtesy, you second-rate hack, you!"

And as I stormed out I asked who that rude man was . . . only Morton da Costa! (*Music Man, Auntie Mame*, etc.)

Avril Lavigne

"I want a big part in a movie . . . I've auditioned twice. Once I got the part and once I didn't. . . . I think it's cool, though, because it's humbling. It's like, ha-ha, I have to start all over again."

Frederick Rolf

Frederick shares this story:

In London, 1946, all wartime restrictions had finally been lifted and I could go after my dream of becoming an actor. I had no professional experience and many rejections, but my first audition was with Sir Lewis Casson, actor and producer and director for many years at the theatre where he was appearing. It took place in his tiny dressing room before the evening performance.

Applying his makeup, he asked me to give him "a taste of your quality." I began with a selection from *Peer Gynt*, as he spread spirit gum on his bald pate you could tell where my concentration was going, three feet away from him. As I approached the climax of the speech he slapped the toupee on his head, turned and said, "Well, you certainly have a lot of power. Now let's hear your comedy."

I said that was all I prepared. "Read something from the book you came in with," he said. "Dante's *The Divine Comedy*?" Fine, read it as if you were Oscar Wilde.

I don't know who fared the worst, Wilde or Dante. "Yes, well, you must work on your upper register. Name?"

"Rolf Frederichs."

"Rather German, isn't it? [Rolf is Jewish.] We'll have to change that." He wrote out a recommendation for . . . Frederick Rolf . . . to a theatre in northern England. My first job as an actor and with a new name. Rolf felt he could conquer the world.

But first he had to work on his upper register.

Richmond Shepard

1. An award-winning mime, Mr. Shepard and a member of his mime troupe some years ago auditioned for the *Ed Sullivan Show*. The casting person sat and watched. When the piece was over, he looked at Mr. Shepard, then shrugged and said, "It's . . . it's . . . it's too *quiet*."

2. Mr. Shepard, up for the part of a transvestite kidnapper on a *Kojak* episode, was told he was called in because as a mime, he would be able to handle the costume. (???!!!)

3. This was a TV show about a blind college professor at a dance who *thinks* he's dancing with a woman, but he's really dancing with a man with whom he speaks. Mr. Shepard, who auditioned and got the part, asked why he got it. They figured he, being a mime, could move *and* speak at the same time! . . . How's that again?

Anonymous

This veteran actor of theatre, film, and TV credits that spanned fifty years appears for an audition. He has the misfortune to be interviewed by a young, know-nothing casting person with a decidedly condescending attitude. "Well, what have you done?"

Slyly, the actor pauses, and with nostrils quivering, asks, "Does it smell that bad?"

Clifton James

Clifton tells this story:

I believe it happened in September 1954. I was sitting in the Theatre Bar on West Forty-Fifth Street when an actor friend told me he had just been cast in a part in a Group Theatre revival, *Johnny Johnson*, and had started rehearsals. He said they were looking for someone to play the mayor and that I would be perfect for the part. He called the director and set up an appointment that very night. I went uptown, around Eightieth and Central Park West, to an elegant apartment. A man dressed to the nines (I thought he was the butler) ushered me into the bedroom and told me to wait.

Soon a beautiful lady in a very sheer negligee came from the bathroom and sat down next to me. She put her hand on my leg, looked deep into my eyes and said, "Clifton, you'll have no trouble with this part. All you will have to do is *think green.*" She told me to be at rehearsal the next day. Then, to the "butler" she called, "Oh, Harold [Clurman, a Group Theatre founder and creative force], show the young man out." I thanked Ms. Stella Adler and left.

Needless to say, one week of rehearsals and I was fired—replaced by Gene Saks—who could obviously *think green* better than I.

Second City / Bernie Sahlins

When actors audition for Second City, the Chicago-based improv group, they're judged on their improvisational ability, stage presence, and sense of timing. Auditions consist of tests like "five-through-the-door," in which the quaking hopeful, without warning, has to concoct five different characters in a row. Do one. Leave. Do the next. Leave. Do another, and so on.

The qualities sought in the inquisition are, first of all, intelligence. According to Second City co-founder Bernie Sahlins, "A know-nothing person who doesn't know who he is, what's going on in the world, or hasn't read anything, I don't use him. Then they have to use their environment, use their fellow actors, use what's on stage. They have to have acting ability, the ability to bring an ironic point of view to what's going on in the world, and stage presence, which is unteachable and undefinable."

Priscilla Lopez

Priscilla shares this story:

Back in '68, before I had an agent, I saw an ad in *Backstage* asking for singers for the new Off-Broadway musical *Hair* that was moving to Broadway. At that point in time I had no idea what *Hair* was, but I went. The audition room was a dance studio with a pianist and a long table with the usual, but unusual, cast of characters sitting behind the table in an almost reclining position. Decked out with their headbands, beads, shirtless mirrored vests, Clorox-stained bell-bottom pants and sandals, the room was filled with smoke as these psychedelic characters smoked their oddly shaped cigarettes. They seemed to be in a natural fog of their own and their movements were quite languid, enjoying some private joke among themselves. Seeing them, I thought, "Why are they dressed so strangely?"

Well, I had shown up in my herringbone hip-hugger mini-mod dress, with zippers on the sleeves, zippers on the hip pockets, zippers on the breast pockets, and a long zipper up the center. I had on white textured stockings, and black patent leather Mary Jane shoes, with a white nylon stretch headband in my hair.

I said hello and gave my music to the pianist. After a couple of bars of introduction, in my most musical comedy persona, from *The Sound of Music* . . . "Raindrops on roses and whiskers on kittens/bright copper kettles and warm woolen mittens. . . ."

Well it was as if the fog in the room started to evaporate quickly, suddenly tense languid figures seem to freeze in disbelief with the exception of their jaws dropping, their stares became fixed and mesmerized. A sight and sound they could not begin to process or absorb. I started to feel something was wrong but I continued with my most Broadwayish presentation, ending with my most powerful vocal ending . . . Silence.

No one moved or stirred, no one said "Thank you," no one said "Don't call us we'll call you." They just remained in their frozen state, staring, most probably thinking that they were on a *bad* acid trip. At that moment I also froze, the only movement being my huge eyeballs shifting back and forth, side to side. I very quietly and slowly tiptoed to the piano, delicately removed my music so as not to awaken them from their frozen stupor, and slipped away.

Bob Ross

Bob tells this story:

I went to an audition for the Burgess Meredith play *Underworld*, where short actors were called. After watching groups of five go out onstage and come back quickly backstage, I realized it was a fast in-and-out. But why five at a time? Anyone shorter than Burgess was kept to read—the other taller ones were dismissed. When I was onstage with my group of five, I placed myself at the end. As Burgess came down the line looking *up* at actors, I knew they were in trouble—so I kept getting shorter as he came closer. By the time he was in front of me he had to look down a few inches to see my eyes. As he glared at me he got shorter, and as he got shorter, I got shorter. As we were heading for Billy Barty time, we both began laughing. He patted my shoulder, as if to say, "Good try, kid," and I was dismissed.

Jerome Robbins / Carol Lawrence

Vying for her first lead on Broadway, Carol was auditioning for Maria in *West Side Story*, directed by Robbins. She got her first taste of Robbins's fearsome style when she endured *twelve* vocal auditions. When he asked her to return for the thirteenth time she summoned up the courage to request reading the balcony scene. He agreed, partnering her with ex-stuntman-turned-actor/singer Larry Kert.

Robbins sent Kert out of the room and told Carol to hide somewhere on stage . . . saying, "Kert will enter singing 'Maria,' then if he can find you, do the balcony scene." The stage was bare, but Carol found a place with a tiny balcony with a ladder on a wall.

Kert entered singing, looking everywhere for her, finished the song, saying, "Maria! Where are you?" Carol impetuously whispers "Tony!" He saw her and almost

Spider-Man-like climbed the wall to her. He clung to her, kissed her, leaped down, finished the song and left.

There wasn't a sound in the theatre. Then, they all stood up and applauded—Arthur Laurents, Stephen Sondheim, the producers. And Leonard Bernstein walked down to the footlights, and said, "That was the most mesmerizing audition I have ever seen in my life. You got it."

Christina Zorich

How to really put your foot in it. This actress was auditioning for a part in a play Off-Broadway called *Spiked Heels*. The character wears spiked heels throughout the play. Christina hardly ever wears them. With a few minutes to kill, she had a coffee nearby, and slips on a pair of four-inch heels figuring it might help. She lurches and weaves across the street to the audition.

The configuration of the theatre was an amphitheater with a rather steep rake from the back of the house to the front of the stage. The actress entered from the top back of the house and proceeded down the stairs to the stage where the director awaited. She nervously took a few steps down in her spiked heels, when she stumbled, tripped and fell at the feet of the director more or less unhurt but somewhat humiliated and laughing hysterically.

After being helped up, she managed to get on stage, still in her spiked heels, and sat on the chair trying to compose herself. Assisting at the audition was an actor hired to read with people. They began. In the scene he had to seductively take off her spiked heels and massage her feet, which he did. The actress, after the rather ignominious fall, began to giggle, then laugh, but trying hard to control herself, just managed to end the scene.

She was thanked, and picking up her spike heels walked out of the theatre in her stockinged feet, a wiser actress.

Alan Bergmann

Bergmann tells this story:

In the early sixties I auditioned for Arthur Penn for a colorful part in *Lorenzo,* a Broadway play starring Alfred Drake. The scene called for me to lead a band of cutthroats in the capture of a troupe of hapless actors. Penn's assistant was reading with me on the large bare stage. As we read, I improvised circling and threatening movements and allowed my anger to increase 'til near the end of the scene, I leaped at the surprised assistant, knocked his script out of his hands, and a hundred pages flew all over the floor.

Arthur hired me on the spot.

I hadn't planned it, but, on reflection, I realized I had seen Arthur's work and his use of violence had lingered in my memory. So, intuitively, I had dared to do the right thing, and it *was* in character.

Richard Herd

Richard shares this story:

It was one of my very first auditions for a Broadway musical. I had prepared two numbers: the upbeat "There Is Nothing Like a Dame," and the ballad "Wonder Why," which Vic Damone sang in the movie *Athena.* I was running the numbers over and over again while waiting in the wings along with some twenty or more others when the stage manager came off-stage, took my music, and told me to wait until he called my name. He did, finally. I took a deep breath, smiled, and walked out onto the vast stage, illuminated by a single, powerful, naked light bulb on a floor stand.

"Richard Herd will be singing 'Wonder Why,'" the stage manager announced to the darkness beyond the apron of the stage, and went over to give the music to the accompanist, who was sitting miles away at the piano, stage right.

I had not reached stage center when a voice boomed out form the darkness of the house, "Thank you, Mr. Herd."

I stopped, stunned, squinted and peered into the darkness of the theatre when I heard again, "Thank you, that's all." Numbed and a bit angry, I somehow managed to cross right to the pianist to pick up my music. As she handed it to me, she said *sotto voce* with a questioning smile and very sweetly the opening words of my song . . . "Wonder why . . . ?"

Jonathan Freeman
Jonathan tells this story:

I once had to be removed from a Broadway stage, weeping uncontrollably.

About twenty years ago—maybe less, it seems like twenty—I auditioned for a new version of *The Merchant of Venice*. It was called *The Merchant* (the show that killed Zero Mostel).

I was told to prepare a "comparable monologue from Shakespeare," so I chose Launcelot Gobbo's monologue from Act 2, Scene 2. Launcelot is Shylock's servant, and in this speech he speaks 1) as the voice of an imaginary friend "at mine elbow," telling him to leave Shylock; 2) as the voice of his conscience, advising him to stay; and 3) in his own voice.

Being young and foolish, I over-prepared and placed far too much importance on the audition.

The scene of the crime was an enormous Broadway stage—I've forgotten which one.

I was very excited.

Hiding somewhere in the back of the house, waiting for his prey, was director John Dexter—a man I shall henceforth refer to as the MMISB, the Meanest Man in Show Business.

After being introduced, I began the monologue. I got off to a shaky start and asked to begin again.

The second time I finished and felt that I had done rather well. There was a long pause. The MMISB spoke.

"Why did you choose this monologue?"

I started to explain and was cut off after a few words.

"Don't you know this is one of the most difficult monologues in all of Shakespeare? What made you think for one moment that you could tackle it?"

I started to explain and was cut off again.

"You are obviously not a student of Shakespeare. Nor will you ever be one at this rate."

He continued berating me until I found myself weeping uncontrollably and had to be led off the stage by the stage manager.

I ran to a pay phone, called my agent and, still sobbing away, told her what had happened.

She consoled me as best she could.

The following day, she phoned and told me I had a call back for *The Merchant* (the show that killed Zero Mostel).

I declined to attend.

Len Lesser

1. While Len was being seen for one film at a movie studio for which he was rejected, a casting person for another film spots him, asks Len to follow him, ushers him into a beautifully appointed office, and tells him to wait. Admiring the pictures on the wall, Len hears a voice with a British accent, turns, and is amazed to see Alfred Hitchcock. They talk about the role of the assassin in *The Man Who Knew Too Much*. As Len leaves, Hitchcock says, "I'll see you on the plane to England."

Len leaves, ecstatic, calls his agent, who says, "I'll go over there tomorrow." Len figures that's what agents do.

Len never got the part and never knew why.

2. Friend Stewart Stern, who had written *Rebel Without a Cause*, recommended Len for it. Len's agent (same one) came with him. Stewart and the producer ok'd Len, but said, "Let's just wait for the director," Nicholas Ray. Len's agent announced, "Oh no, we don't wait for no one, come on, Len." Outside, the agent says to Len, "The first thing you learn in this town, kid, is don't wait for anybody."

On the phone later, Stewart asks, "What the hell is wrong with that guy? They won't touch you now with a ten-foot pole."

Len didn't get that part either. Afterwards, he learned his agent all the while was having a *nervous breakdown* and was being treated at a sanitorium.

Kate Buddeke

Auditioning for the part of Mazeppa, the trumpet-playing stripper in the 2003 production of the musical *Gypsy* ("If you want to bump it, bump it with a trumpet"), Kate was a bit early, so before going in she was having a cigarette and a cup of coffee outside, in front of the theatre, when Sam Mendes, the show's director, walked by, stopped, and said, "That's Mazeppa!"

Sam was right . . . but instead of a trumpet, Kate plays a bugle.

Dennis Creaghan

Dennis is reading for a play. He finishes. The director says, "Can you play it shorter?"

"Shorter?" asks Dennis, "You mean compressed, tighten it up?"

"How tall are you?" the director asks.

Dennis: "Five-ten."

"The character is five-five . . . can you play shorter?'

Mario Lanza

An army training camp in the 1940s. NCO Johnny Silver, an ex–burlesque comic, was going over service records in search of talent for future touring variety shows. One young private's record looked promising. Silver brought him in to sing and was so impressed, he launched a campaign to keep him out of combat, getting him reassigned as a chaplain's assistant.

Visiting Sgt. Peter Lind Hayes was auditioning for the musical *On the Beam*. Unfortunately, the young private had an inflamed throat and couldn't sing. Silver got to work. He pasted a second label on a disk featuring a Met Opera tenor, identifying it as the young private. Hayes heard the record and was bowled over.

The young private, Mario Lanza, then Cocozza, joined the cast and became the audience's favorite . . . the "Caruso of the Air Force."

David Gardner

1. David shares this story:

I was suspicious from the start. Before the audition they asked me to sign some kind of waiver that if I got the job I couldn't do any other commercials for ten years and, if I remember correctly, any other acting either. I declined that little "exclusive services" gambit with a smile, saying, "Let's just see if I get the part first."

The script was cheery. I was asked to be that nice-looking squared-jawed guy with the white hair standing at the curb in front of his picket fence, holding up a super-strong garbage bag (Glad). The words: "It sure feels great to be assured that your garbage bag . . . etc." They wanted me to wear a white wig that was much too small, and as I tugged on it I wondered how many others had worn it already in this nationwide search to find the right Mr. Glad.

At the taping, the room was filled with executive decisionmakers sitting behind a table laden with half-eaten food, their eyes glued to the monitor. I begin: "Well, it sure feels great to be assured that . . . that [pause] . . . this filthy unfitting piece of garbage [the words just poured out] . . . makes me look and feel like an absolute idiot!"

I whipped off the offending wig and threw it on the floor. The camera stopped . . . a pregnant *hari kari* hush filled the room. I mumbled "thank you" and walked purposefully out.

Needless to say, I never worked for that ad agency again, but it felt good to be honest, at least once, in a commercial audition.

2. The commercial was for the Toronto real estate board, and David was auditioning for its spokesperson. The idea behind the spot was that the television viewer and the actor literally put themselves *inside* a house and *imagined* what it was like to live there. Well and good, except when David came to the audition he was given an actual model bungalow to place over his head, putting himself "inside the house" and getting to know "what it was like to live there." And there he was . . . looking out through the upstairs windows and talking through the front door.

David thought he did a heads-up job: he didn't get claustrophobic and he didn't freak out, and he can't imagine why he didn't become the in-house spokesperson for the *real* estate board.

Linda Goranson

Linda Goranson tells this story:

A few years ago I heard of a part in a play I wanted very badly to do. I fought for an audition and got it. I chose my wardrobe very carefully and did some heavy dark eye makeup I felt was right for the character. I felt good about

myself, auditioned, and waited for a reaction. The director spoke: "Linda, I brought you here because I thought
you could bring something new and wonderful to the part.
Obviously you can't. So thank you very much."

I was so shocked, I stumbled to the door, opened, and
closed it. When I realized I had walked into the broom
closet, I burst into tears. In the state I was in, I couldn't
go out. I decided to wait him out, wait until he went away.
I couldn't stop sobbing and my tears were smearing the
black eye makeup. I knew he knew I was in the closet, but I
was determined not to come out until he was gone. Finally
I realized he was not going to leave . . . other people were
auditioning . . . I *had* to come out. I cracked the door. He
was there sitting behind the desk staring at the door waiting
to see how long I'd remain in the closet. He stared at my
black streaky face.

I had pulled myself together, but I could barely speak. "I
got the wrong . . . room."

"I know."

"So, where's the door?"

He pointed . . . and I left.

George Guidall

Reggie Jackson, the one-time New York Yankees star, was,
for a while, the TV spokesman for Panasonic cameras, video
cameras, etc.

One of the spots involved Reggie demonstrating the
product to a prospective buyer.

Every actor in New York auditioned for that part with
Reggie; "Mr. October" was widely popular.

George Guidall was the lucky one. Delighted to be doing
the spot, but a bit puzzled, George wondered why he, of all
the actors, literally hundreds, was chosen.

He was told that when viewing the actors on the audition tapes, they felt George looked like he was the easiest to get along with.

Louis Zorich

Called in to read for a running part on a highly rated soap opera in New York, I was pleasantly surprised to be warmly greeted by a classmate from drama school, a one-time actor, now producer. We talked briefly about the "good old days" and mutual friends. Unfortunately, I wasn't a habitual viewer of his show; nevertheless, he clued me in on the role: "He's a Zorba-like character." I thanked him for his help, grateful that the "old school ties" connection was alive and well.

I plunged into the audition, creating a powerful and riveting performance. I called my agent for good news. It wasn't. In shock, I asked why.

"They thought you were too passionate and arrogant."

"But," I insisted, "that's what they wanted."

"I'm sorry, that's what they said."

It didn't make sense.

Years later, I ran into the same classmate-producer friend and somehow the Zorba audition came up. Obviously it still puzzled and disturbed me, since a well-known casting lady once told me I was made to play Zorba, that larger-than-life, passionate, free-spirited Greek who lusted for life, women, song, and dance. My friend looked at me strangely, "Aha! No wonder," he said, "Not *that* Zorba. I meant the kind, old Dr. Zorba on the *Ben Casey* TV show."

Jay Thomas

1. Jay went to see a producer about a job; at the appointed time he walked into the office, but didn't see anyone. He heard a woman's voice, and then saw the woman's head poking up from behind the desk. She was on the floor. Jay greeted her, and when the woman stood up, Jay realized she was about eight months pregnant. She said her back was killing her. Jay told her it was ok. She asked if he was sure, he wouldn't at all mind?

Jay nodded.

She lay back down on the floor, from where she conducted the interview.

2. The star of a TV show, a young comedienne, along with her producer, were auditioning Jay to play her husband on the show. At the time, Jay was hot and he was pretty sure he was going to get the job. However, the "word" was that she had a bad reputation . . . difficult to work with. Actually, she and Jay got along famously—they talked, they laughed a lot, and things were going great. Suddenly, the producer stood up and said, "I've got to say this . . . you two . . . you two together as I've been watching, you two would just jump off the screen if you played her husband. I'm going to phone the network president right *now* and tell him I got Jay Thomas in here and tell him what I'm seeing."

He called for his secretary and told her to get Les Moonves on the phone. Jay was saying that it wasn't necessary, etc., etc. The producer was saying, no, no, I'm doing it right now. The secretary returned, informed the producer that she had the network president, Les Moonves, on the line. The producer said he'd be right back and left the room.

Jay was sitting there with the casting people and the star comedienne, and he said "Wouldn't it be funny if he mentions my name to Les and Les says, 'What? Are you kidding? I wouldn't have that guy on my network on a bet!'" Everybody broke up.

The door opened and the producer returned, looked at Jay, and said, "Ah . . . I'll tell you what, Jay, I'm going to have to call you back."

3. Jay shares this story:

I was up for the original episode of what was to become one of the top-rated sitcoms. The part: a Pulitzer Prize–winning writer, misogynistic and sarcastic, who really comes on to the star, but is frustrated so he starts to put her down. That was the premise of the character. One of the producers promoted me, and my agent fought for me. So I said to myself, "I'm going to *be* the character!"

Present were the network execs, the producers, director, and casting people, and I start attacking them, particularly the director. "We worked together in New York City . . . you couldn't direct a dying scene if you'd given the actors poison!" I went after them. I was killing them. . . . I mean, I was vicious . . . and I leave the room.

At home later, my friend the producer calls, "What the hell did you do?" Jay explained that he *was* the character the moment he stepped into the room. "They hated your guts! . . . They don't want you on the lot! . . . You were so awful. They never ever want to see you again!"

Jay: "Are you kidding? My God, I was joking!"

"You're lucky you got a radio job, you're finished at Warner Bros.!"

Shortly after, my agent calls, "You insulted the director, you were sarcastic to the other people," and on and on.

A year or two later this very same show is a big, big hit. On it is this character, Jerry Gold, an evil, right-wing, Jewish announcer type, who's always saying mean and nasty things. . . . You never see him, you only hear about him. . . . He's talked about. Oddly enough, the character becomes wildly popular, so much that viewers are writing in. They want to *see* Jerry Gold. The creative people are saying, "We gotta get somebody in here, but who?"

"Remember that a****** who came in here a few years ago? Call Jay Thomas."

My agent calls and says, "They are asking for you, they must have forgotten what you did.'"

I said, "I can't go, I can't, no way."

"But they *really* want to see you!"

I get the script. This Jerry Gold is a phony TV guy. He's not the same character I originally did, but I go in anyway. Everybody is there . . . same people, the same director. I'm very nice with them all . . . very nice. I read. They look at me with a "What the hell was that?" look. "No, no, no . . . we want that guy you did two years ago, saying those things you said to the director . . . *that's* the guy we want!"

I did all the stuff I did two years ago. They hired me for one show, then off and on for seven years.

I won two Emmys.

4. The situation: a new TV drama that is creating a lot of stir, in other words, it's touted to be a winner. The character Jay is auditioning for is someone who is tough and candid who runs the White House and knows everything about everyone. Jay, outside going over the script, looks up and sees an actor friend coming out of the office. His friend is young and handsome and sweating. It seems he's read three or four times now and definitely feels he's got the part. After congratulating him, Jay goes in. They have a little conversation. Jay tells them they have a great cast lined up . . . then someone asks, "Why, what have you heard?"

Jay mentions that he just finished talking to the young hunk who left, and he thinks he'd be perfect for the show.

Director: "Why do you think that?"

Jay: "Because he has a huge cock."

The place breaks up. Someone says "You sound like you know him better than you're letting on."

Jay: "Oh, come on. We all saw that video with him in a hotel room. . . . He's huge." And Jay is demonstrating. The casting director is laughing. But the director's face is frozen . . . he doesn't move.

He reads, they thank him, and he leaves.

The next day, it hits the fan. Jay's agent is on the phone.

"What the hell is going on? You were set for a callback, you were on their short list, but now they do not want to see you ever."

Jay tells him exactly what happened.

Agent: "Oh my God! That director has no sense of humor . . . and there were women in the room. That's it for you, buddy."

By now, Jay is embarrassed and humiliated. He tells his wife the whole story.

"Are we going to have to move again?" she asks.

Shelley Winters

Shelley Winters was asked to audition for a film. She entered the producer's office and sat in a chair directly in front of his desk. He started right in on the importance of the project and of casting the right people in the right roles a ya da ya da ya da. After a while, Shelley Winters leaned over, pulled an Oscar out of her bag and set it on his desk. The producer stopped for a moment, then went on telling her about the movie. She reached down and pulled a second Oscar out of her bag. Finally the producer stopped.

And Miss Winters said, "Some people think I can act."

Kirk Douglas

Kirk was making a screen test for his first film, *The Strange Love of Martha Ivers*. The director was Lewis Milestone, who directed *The Front Page* and *Of Mice and Men*, and who won the Academy Award for *All Quiet on the Western Front*. He gave Kirk the script and let him rehearse his scene four or five times. When he finished, Kirk said he was ready for the test.

Milestone said, "Go home. I've been filming all along. You got the part."

Clint Eastwood

In the early fifties, Universal Pictures was making screen tests of actors for possible appearances in 3-D films. Clint wanted to see what he looked like, so he went and was tested. The test was simple—stand up, sit down, turn left, turn right, walk around, look at the camera, tell us a little about yourself. All of which he did.

A few days later, he went back to the studio, looked at the tests, and said, "Boy, am I in trouble."

William Andrew Jones

William Andrew Jones shares this story:

My audition reminiscence goes all the way back to college, when I appeared in Shaw's *The Devil's Desciple*, starring and directed by the noted British actor Sir Cyril Ritchard. The day of the callbacks, the ten of us who had been given speaking parts were seated in the house (feeling very pleased with ourselves, I must admit). On stage were seventy or eighty fellow students, about to be cast as British soldiers, townspeople, Indians, etc.

When it came time to cast the Indians, Sir Ritchard had all the men line up and take off their shirts, since some of the Indians would be scantily clad. He then reviewed the troops, slowly walking down the line, checking them out, each and every one.

As he continued his inspection, one of the actors in the house whispered, "Monday . . . Tuesday . . . Wednesday . . ."

David Niven

Director Frank Capra was about to start his next film project, *Lost Horizon*, with Ronald Colman as the lead. Colman, a friend of Niven's, suggested to Capra that Niven would be very right for the part of Colman's brother. Capra met with Niven and wasn't that convinced, but he told Niven he'd give him a screen test in a week or so.

Niven waited. For six days. No calls. He figured it wasn't going to happen. He went fishing with some friends, but just in case Capra would call he had someone back at the house to get the call. The plan was then to signal Niven on the fishing boat by driving to Malibu Heights and to wave a white sheet for Niven to see.

Niven's fishing buddies were apprised of the situation. All were keeping an eye out for the flapping sheet. The fishing went well. The captain wondered how Niven would get to the shore.

"I'll swim," said Niven, "It's only a couple of hundred yards."

The captain corrected him, saying, "More like five."

Later, as the boat got closer to shore, Niven spotted the sheet being waved. He immediately stripped down to his shorts and dove into the water heading toward the shore. As he stroked he soon hit the kelp beds, which reached out quite a distance. It was tricky to get past the beds without getting entangled in them, for their roots extended to the ocean floor. Niven managed to get past and through the beds. The ocean was rough and got rougher as he swam. Niven began to be hit by the waves, being tossed around and up and down, touching bottom, then being propelled up again. His mouth and nose were filled with sand and water. Suddenly he was swept up by a wave and dumped on the shore, bruised and shaken up. With help he was driven home.

Relieved and somewhat worse for the wear, he phoned Capra's office and was told that Capra had left for the day by his secretary, who said to Niven, "Oh, you shouldn't have rushed back from your fishing. Mr. Capra just wanted to tell you that he will not be making your test because he has cast John Howard in the part."

Author Biography

Broadway: *Becket* (with Laurence Olivier, Anthony Quinn); *Moby Dick* (Rod Steiger); *Odd Couple* (Walter Matthau, Art Carney); Lincoln Center Rep. (Herbert Blau, Jules Irving), *Danton's Death*; *Country Wife*; *Condemned of Altona*; *Hadrian VII* (Tony nomination); *Fun City* (Joan Rivers); *Goodtime Charley* (Joel Grey, Ann Reinking); *Herzl*; *Moon Children*; *They Knew What They Wanted* (Drama Desk nomination); *Death of a Salesman* (Dustin Hoffman); *Arms and the Man* (Kevin Kline, Raul Julia); *Marriage Of Figaro* (Chris Reeve); *She Loves Me.*

Encore Series: *On a Clear Day You Can See Forever.*

Voices Series: *Little Murders*; *Follies* (Blythe Danner, Judith Ivey); *45 Seconds from Broadway*; *Ma Rainey's Black Bottom* (Whoopi Goldberg, Charles S. Dutton).

Films: *Hole in One*; *Friends and Family*; *Commandments*; *Fish in the Bathtub*; *City of Hope*; *Muppets Take Manhattan*; *Fiddler on the Roof*; *The Don Is Dead*; *Newman's Law*; *Honor Thy Father.*

Television Series: *Brooklyn Bridge*; *Mad About You.* Over 350 TV shows in both the U.S. and Canada. Over 100 TV commercials (on camera and voice overs).

Off-Broadway: *Henry IV, Parts I & II* (as Falstaff); *The Tempest*; *Henry V*; *True West* (Tommy Lee Jones, Peter Boyle); *Medea*; *The Thracian Horses*; *Good Soldier Schweik*; *Crimes and Crimes*; *The Size of the World*; *Six Characters in Search of an Author*; *Oedipus* (Al Pacino); *To Clothe the Naked*; *Sunset.*

Regional Theatres: Williamstown Summer Theatre; McCarter (Princeton, N.J.); New Harmony (Indiana); Studio Theatre (Buffalo); Stratford (Canada); Crest (Toronto); Goodman (Chicago); Delaware Theatre Co. American Stage (Milford, N.H.); Pacific Coast Rep. Studebaker Theatre Co. (Chicago); Whole Theatre Co. (Montclair, N.J., 18 years).

Sources and Permissions

Chapter One: You Won't Believe This

Meryl Streep: Linson, Art. 1993. *A Pound of Flesh: Perilous Tales of How to Produce Movies in Hollywood.* Grove Press. Copyright © 1993 by Art Linson. Used by permission of Grove/Atlantic, Inc.

Calista Flockhart: *The Tonight Show* with Jay Leno and *National Enquirer,* April 13, 1999.

Robert Mitchum: Server, Lee. 2002. *Robert Mitchum: "Baby I Don't Care."* St. Martin's Press.

Richard Rodgers: Hyland, William G. 1998. *Richard Rodgers.* Yale University Press.

Federico Fellini: Eastman, John. 1989. *Retakes.* Ballantine Books. Used with permission.

Kevin Spacey: *Entertainment Weekly,* January 4, 2002.

Klaus Kinski: Kinski, Klaus. 1997. *Kinski Uncut: The Autobiography of Klaus Kinski.* Translated from German by Joachim Neugroshel. Penguin Books.

Michael Gambon: Gussow, Mel. 2004. *A Life in Acting.* Applause Theatre & Cinema Books.

Marlon Brando: Brando, A. K. and E. P. Stein. 1980. *Brando for Breakfast.* Berkley Books.

Gary Merrill: As told to Louis Zorich by Mason Adams.

Oliver Stone: As told to Louis Zorich by Julius Tennon.

Peter Riegert: As told to Louis Zorich by Peter Riegert.

Renée Zellweger: *New York Times,* September 10, 2000.

Theodore Komisarjevsky: Gielgud, J. and C. N. Potter. 1980. *An Actor and His Time.*

Susan Sarandon: *New York Post,* November 7, 1999.

William Youmans: As told to Louis Zorich by William Youmans.

Bijou Phillips: *Talk Magazine,* April 2000.

Gower Champion: Hunt, Gordon. 1995. *How to Audition: For TV, Movies, Commercials, Plays, and Musicals.* Harper Collins.

Paul Mazursky: Mazursky, Paul. 1999. *Show Me the Magic.* Simon & Schuster.

Michael Caine: Freedland, Michael. 1999. *Michael Caine.* Thorndike Press.

Andre Gregory: *American Theatre Magazine*, March 2005.

Alec Guinness: *Talk Magazine*, September 1999.

Celeste Holm: As told to Louis Zorich by Louis Negin.

Robert Kalfin: As told to Louis Zorich by Robert Kalfin.

Joe Sicardi: As told to Louis Zorich by Joe Sicardi.

Judi Dench: Miller, John. 1997. *Judi Dench: With a Crack in Her Voice.* Orion Non-Fiction, an imprint of The Orion Publishing Group, London. Used with permission.

Treat Williams: As told to Louis Zorich by Treat Williams.

Betty Garrett: Garrett, B. and R. Rapoport. 1998. *Betty Garrett and Other Songs: A Life on Stage and Screen.* Madison Books. Used with permission.

Lerner & Loewe: Bach, Steven. 2001. *Dazzler: The Life & Times of Moss Hart.* Knopf. Used with permission.

Hal Prince: As told to Louis Zorich by Robert Kalfin.

Ginger Rogers: Hadleigh, Boze. 1998. *Hollywood and Whine: The Snippy, Snotty, and Scandalous Things Stars Say About Each Other.* Birch Lane Press.

Gerry Jedd: Hunt, Gordon. 1995. *How to Audition: For TV, Movies, Commercials, Plays, and Musicals.* Harper Collins.

David Black: Black, David. 1990. *The Actor's Audition.* Vintage Books.

Jack Davidson: As told to Louis Zorich by Jack Davidson.

Malachy McCourt: Coffey, Michael. 1997. *The Irish in America.* Hyperion.

James Cavanaugh: As told to Louis Zorich by James Cavanaugh.

William Devane: Tartikoff, B. and C. Leerhsen. 1992. *The Last Great Ride.* Turtle Bay Books. Used with permission.

George London: *Opera News*, November 2001, Vol. 66, #5.

Rocco Sisto: As told to Louis Zorich by Rocco Sisto.

Josh Logan: Randall, T. and M. Mindlin. 1989. *Which Reminds Me.* Delacorte Press.

Josef Sommer: As told to Louis Zorich by Josef Sommer.

Jack Klugman: As told to Louis Zorich by Jack Klugman.

Barry Moss: Hunt, Gordon. 1995. *How to Audition: For TV, Movies, Commercials, Plays, and Musicals.* Harper Collins.

Timothy Carey: Biskind, Peter. 1998. *Easy Riders, Raging Bulls.* Simon & Schuster.

Dame Peggy Ashcroft: As told to Louis Zorich by Simon Jones.

Roscoe Lee Browne: As told to Louis Zorich by Roscoe Lee Browne.

Larry Block: As told to Louis Zorich by Larry Block.

Stephen Moorer: As told to Louis Zorich by Stephen Moorer.

Peter Von Berg: As told to Louis Zorich by Peter Von Berg.

Chapter Two: What?

Mel Gibson: Smith, Liz. *New York Post,* July 30, 2004.

Audrey Hepburn: Vadim, Roger. 1986. *Bardot, Deneuve, Fonda: An Autobiography.* Simon & Schuster.

Paul Muni: Hay, Peter. 1987. *Theatrical Anecdotes.* Oxford University Press. Used with permission.

Dustin Hoffman: As told to Louis Zorich by Dustin Hoffman.

Pamela Payton-Wright: As told to Louis Zorich by Pamela Payton-Wright.

George C. Scott: As told to Louis Zorich by Zelda Fischandler.

Paul Scofield: O'Connor, Gary. 2002. *Paul Scofield: An Actor For All Seasons.* Applause Books.

The Beatles: As told to Louis Zorich.

Allen Blumenfeld: As told to Louis Zorich.

David Mamet: As told to Louis Zorich.

Alex Rocco: As told to Louis Zorich by Alex Rocco.

Spalding Gray: Shewey, Don and Susan Shacter. 1986. *Caught in the Act: New York Actors Face to Face.* New American Library. Used with permission.

Lew Wasserman: Bruck, Connie. 2003. *When Hollywood Had a King,* Random House. Used with permission.

Ray Walston: 1. As told to Louis Zorich by Fyvush Finkel. **2.** Chandler, Charlotte. 2002. *Nobody's Perfect: Billy Wilder: A Personal Biography.* Simon & Schuster. **3.** As told to Louis Zorich by Fyvush Finkel.

Lehman Engel: As told to Louis Zorich by Rod Derenfinko.

Ron McClarty: As told to Louis Zorich by Ron McClarty.

Richard Pryor: Pryor, R. and T. Gold. 1995. *Pryor Convictions, and Other Life Sentences.* Pantheon Books.

Noel Coward: Lillie, B., J. Philip, and J. Brough. 1974. *Every Other Inch a Lady.* Dell Publishing.

James Komack: Kleiner, Dick. 1981. *Please Don't Shoot My Dog: The Autobiography of Jackie Cooper.*

Margaret Whitton: As told to Louis Zorich by Margaret Whitton.

Jack Warden: Grodin, Charles. 1989. *It Would Be So Nice If You Weren't Here.* Vintage Books.

Tony Lo Bianco: As told to Louis Zorich by Tony Lo Bianco.

Gary Merrill: Merrill, Gary. 1990. *Bette, Rita and the Rest of My Life.* Berkley Publishing Group.

Charlton Heston: As told to Louis Zorich by Gerald Hiken.

Dorothy Dandridge: Adams, Cindy. *New York Post,* September 24, 1999.

Jon Voight: As told to Louis Zorich by Jon Voight.

Robert De Niro: As told to Louis Zorich by Alan Willig.

Woody Allen: Hay, Peter. 1992. *Canned Laughter: The Best Stories from Radio and Television.* Oxford University Press. Used with permission.

Larry Bryggman: As told to Louis Zorich by Larry Bryggman.

Charles Bronson: Obituary of Charles Bronson, *New York Times,* September 2, 2003.

Jane Curtin: Hill, Douglas. 1987. *Saturday Night: A Backstage History of* Saturday Night Live. Vintage Books.

Sam Spiegel, Montgomery Clift, Peter O'Toole: Sinclair, Andrew. 1987. *Spiegel: The Man Behind the Pictures.* Little, Brown & Co.

Ethan Phillips: As told to Louis Zorich by Ethan Phillips.

Walter Beakel: As told to Louis Zorich by Walter Beakel.

William Duell: As told to Louis Zorich by William Duell.

Morley Safer: Hay, Peter. 1992. *Canned Laughter: The Best Stories from Radio and Television.* Oxford University Press. Used with permission.

Faith Prince: *New York Post*, April 8, 2001.

Anonymous: As told to Louis Zorich by Bill Jones.

Marsha Mason: Mason, Marsha. 2001. *Journey: A Personal Odyssey.* Simon & Schuster.

Armin Shimerman: As told to Louis Zorich by Armin Shimerman.

Philip Seymour Hoffman: *Time Magazine*, November 22, 1999.

Don Francks: Green, Lynda Mason and Tedde Moore, comp. and ed. 1997. *Standing Naked in the Wings: Anecdotes from Canadian Actors.* Oxford University Press. Used with permission.

Roddy McDowell: Kleiner, Dick. 1981. *Please Don't Shoot My Dog: The Autobiography of Jackie Cooper.* Berkley Books.

Kim Hunter: As told to Louis Zorich by Kim Hunter.

Kim Stanley: 1. Kobal, John. 1986. *People Will Talk.* Knopf. Used with permission. **2.** As told to Louis Zorich by Kim Stanley.

Brenda Fricker: As told to Louis Zorich by Brenda Fricker.

Karl Malden: As told to Louis Zorich by Karl Malden.

Rudolph Valentino: *New York Times Book Review*, May 11, 2003.

Hume Cronyn: Obituary of Hume Cronyn, *New York Times.*

Marlene Dietrich: Hay, Peter. 1991. *Movie Anecdotes.* Oxford University Press. Used with permission.

Malcolm Black: As told to Louis Zorich by Malcolm Black.

George Sperdakos: As told to Louis Zorich by George Sperdakos.

Carol Teitel: As told to Louis Zorich by Carol Teitel.

Michael O'Sullivan: As told to Louis Zorich by Michael O'Sullivan.

Chapter Three: Get the Job

Madonna: Medavoy, M. and J. Young. 2002. *You're Only as Good as Your Next One.* Pocket Books.

William H. Macy: *National Public Radio*, 2001. Used with permission.

Rosie O'Donnell: *Actors Equity News*, October 7, 2003. Used with permission.

Gregory Peck: As told to Louis Zorich by Bill Jones.

Oprah Winfrey: Thomas, Marlo. 2002. *The Right Words at the Right Time.* Atria Books.

Jerry Stiller: Stiller, Jerry, 2000. *Married to Laughter.* Simon & Schuster.

Peter Sellers: Sikov, Ed. 2002. *Mr. Strangelove: A Biography of Peter Sellers.* Hyperion.

James Caan: Harper Entertainment, New York.

Richard Harris: As told to Louis Zorich by Jared Harris.

Charlize Theron: *Time Magazine,* October 30, 2000.

Whoopi Goldberg: Parrish, Robert James. 1997. *Whoopi Goldberg: Her Journey from Poverty to Megastardom.* Birch Lane Press.

Howie Mandel: Richmond, Ray. 1999. *My Greatest Day in Show Business.* Taylor Publishing. Used with permission.

Danny Aiello: As told to Louis Zorich by Danny Aiello.

Anthony Quinn: Quinn, A. and D. Paisner. 1995. *One Man Tango.* Harper Collins. Used with permission.

Gregory Hines: Shewey, Don and Susan Shacter. 1986.*Caught in the Act: New York Actors Face to Face.* New American Library. Used with permission.

Warren Beatty: Munshower, Suzanne. 1983. *Warren Beatty: His Life, His Loves, His Work.* St. Martin's Press.

Adam Sandler: Miller, J. A. and T. Shales. 2002. *Live From New York: An Uncensored History of* Saturday Night Live. Little, Brown & Co. Used with permission.

Danny DeVito: *Emmy Magazine,* Stan Rosenfield.

Dabney Coleman: Tartikoff, B. and C. Leerhsen. 1992. *The Last Great Ride.* Turtle Bay Books. Used with permission.

Camryn Manheim: *US Magazine,* 1999.

Jackie Cooper: Cooper, J. and Kleiner, D. 1981. *Please Don't Shoot My Dog.* Berkley Books.

Mitch Ryan: As told to Louis Zorich by Paul Jenkins.

Bea Lillie: Lillie, B., J. Philip, and J. Brough. 1974. *Every Other Inch a Lady.* Dell Publishing.

Margaret Hall: As told to Louis Zorich by Margaret Hall.

Abe Vigoda: *New York Times,* March 25, 2001.

Lee Wilkof: As told to Louis Zorich by Lee Wilkof.

Ron Liebman: As told to Louis Zorich by Ron Liebman.

Roy Scheider: Shewey, Don and Susan Shacter. 1986. *Caught in the Act: New York Actors Face to Face*. New American Library. Used with permission.

Sean Hayes: *Entertainment Weekly*, 1995.

Joe Viterelli: *The Wayne Brady Show.*

Kirk Douglas: Kramer, S. and T. M. Coffey. 1997. *It's a Mad, Mad, Mad, Mad World*. Harcourt Brace.

Anthony Mackie: As told to Louis Zorich by Anthony Mackie.

Joe Morton: As told to Louis Zorich by Joe Morton.

Sheldon Leonard: Leonard, Sheldon. 1995. *And the Show Goes On: Broadway and Hollywood Adventures*. Limelight.

Warren Oates: Matson, Katinka. 1976. *The Working Actor*. Viking.

Peter Hunt: Hunt, Gordon. 1995. *How to Audition: For TV, Movies, Commercials, Plays, and Musicals*. Harper Collins.

William Duell: As told to Louis Zorich by William Duell.

Estelle Getty: *Daily Variety*, June 23, 2008.

Chapter Four: Nervous?

Will Ferrell: *Emmy Magazine*, Vol. XXIII, #3.

Anthony Hopkins: Falk, Quentin. 1994. *Anthony Hopkins: The Authorized Biography*. Published by Interlink Books, an imprint of Interlink Publishing Group, Inc. Text copyright © Quentin Falk, 1989, 1994. Reprinted by permission.

Elaine Stritch: As told to Louis Zorich by Elaine Stritch.

Jack Black: *New York Times Magazine*, September 28, 2003.

Stephen Sondheim: As told to Louis Zorich by Jeff Saver.

Gene Wilder: Brown, Jared. 1989. *Zero Mostel: A Biography*. Atheneum.

Alfred Lunt: As told to Louis Zorich by Jacqueline Bertrand.

David Hasselhoff: Frankel, Terrie Maxine. 1996. *You'll Never Make Love in This Town Again*. Dove Books.

Joan Rivers: Rivers, J. and R. Marryman. 1991. *Still Talking.* Random House, Turtle Bay Books.

F. Murray Abraham: As told to Louis Zorich by F. Murray Abraham.

Audra McDonald: As told to Louis Zorich by Eric Stern.

Ralph Richardson: Miller, John. 1997. *Ralph Richardson: The Authorized Biography.* Trafalgar Square Publishing.

Olympia Dukakis: As told to Louis Zorich by Olympia Dukakis.

Terrence Stamp: *New York Times,* October 3, 1999.

Judy Blazer: As told to Louis Zorich by Judy Blazer.

John Frankenheimer: As told to Louis Zorich by Fred Coffin.

Tyne Daly: As told to Louis Zorich by Stuart Howard.

David Schwimmer: *National Enquirer,* March 15, 1999.

Dustin Hoffman: As told to Louis Zorich by Dustin Hoffman.

Hermione Gingold: Sondheim, S. and M. Secrest. 1998. *Stephen Sondheim: A Life.* Knopf. Used with permission.

Ivor Novello: Milton, F. 1985. *Name Dropping.* E. P. Dutton.

Anonymous: As told to Louis Zorich.

Nikos Psacharopoulos: As told to Louis Zorich by Nikos Psacharopoulos.

Bob Heller: As told to Louis Zorich by Bob Heller.

Paul Mazursky: Mazursky, Paul. 1999. *Show Me the Magic.* Simon & Schuster.

Fred Coffin: As told to Louis Zorich by Fred Coffin.

Chapter Five: When One Door Opens . . .

Marilyn Monroe: Bacon, James. 1976. *Hollywood Is a Four Letter Town.* Avon Books.

Jay Leno: Leno, J. and B. Zehme. 1996. *Leading with My Chin.* Harper Collins.

Jennifer Lopez: Hadleigh, Boze. 1998. *Hollywood and Whine: The Snippy, Snotty, and Scandalous Things Stars Say About Each Other.* Birch Lane Press. Used with permission.

Peter Boyle: McCrohan, Donna. 1987. *The Second City: A Backstage History of Comedy's Hottest Troupe.* Perigee Books.

George Grizzard: *The Soul of the American Actor.*

Fred Astaire: As told to Louis Zorich by Bill Jones.

Jack Nicholson: Siegel, B. and S. Siegel. 1990. *Jack Nicholson: The Unauthorized Biography*. Avon Books.

Bette Davis: *National Enquirer*, December 21, 1999.

James Cagney: As told to Louis Zorich by Howard Rollins.

Ava Gardner: *National Enquirer*, December 21, 1999.

Brad Davis: As told to Louis Zorich by Bill Jones.

Faye Dunaway: Munshower, Suzanne. 1983. *Warren Beatty: His Life, His Loves, His Work*. St. Martin's Press.

Charles Grodin: Grodin, Charles. 1989. *It Would Be So Nice If You Weren't Here*. Vintage Books.

Shirley MacLaine: Lawrence, Greg. 2002. *Dance with Demons: The Life of Jerome Robbins*. G. P. Putnam & Sons. Used with permission.

Neil Simon: Louis Zorich's audition for the film *The Out-of-Towners* with director Arthur Hiller.

Spencer Tracy: Swindell, Larry. 1969. *Spencer Tracy: A Biography*. New American Library.

Kenneth Mars: *Vanity Fair*, January 2004.

Don Knotts: Knotts, D. and R. Metz. 1999. *Barney Fife and Other Characters I Have Known*. Berkley Boulevard Publishing.

Laurence Olivier: Spoto, Donald. 2001. *Laurence Olivier*. Harper Collins.

Fred Gwynne: Tartikoff, B. and C. Leerhsen. 1992. *The Last Great Ride*. Turtle Bay Books. Used with permission.

Henry Fonda: As told to Louis Zorich by Michael J. Bloom.

Jane Powell: As told to Louis Zorich by Jerry Adler.

John Cassavetes: As told to Louis Zorich by Harry Mastrogeorge.

Patti LuPone: *Theatre Week Magazine*, December 30, 1996.

Louis Zorich: As told by Louis Zorich.

Stanley Kramer: Kramer, S. and T. M. Coffey. 1997. *It's a Mad, Mad, Mad, Mad World*. Harcourt Brace.

Alberta Watson: Green, Lynda Mason and Tedde Moore, comp. and ed. 1997. *Standing Naked in the Wings: Anecdotes from Canadian Actors*. Oxford University Press.

Judith Light: Richmond, Ray. 1999. *My Greatest Day in Show Business.* Taylor Publishing. Used with permission.

Clark Gable: Hay, Peter. 1991. *Movie Anecdotes.* Oxford University Press. Used with permission.

Polly Bergen: *Playbill,* Harry Haun, 2001.

Anonymous: As told to Louis Zorich.

Tyrone Power: Arce, Hector. 1980. *The Secret Life of Tyrone Power.* Bantam Books.

Jackson Beck: *Aftra Magazine,* Fall 2004.

Hobe Nelson: As told to Louis Zorich by Lynn Lentz.

Barry Primus: As told to Louis Zorich by Barry Primus.

Joey Sorge: As told to Louis Zorich by Joey Sorge.

William Youmans: As told to Louis Zorich by William Youmans.

James Cavanaugh: As told to Louis Zorich by James Cavanaugh.

Lily Tomlin: Sorenson, Jeff. 1989. *Lily Tomlin: Woman of a Thousand Faces.* St. Martin's Press.

Anonymous: As told to Louis Zorich.

Juliet Taylor: Hunt, Gordon. 1995. *How to Audition: For TV, Movies, Commercials, Plays, and Musicals.* Harper Collins.

Robin Gammell: Green, Lynda Mason and Tedde Moore, comp. and ed. 1997. *Standing Naked in the Wings: Anecdotes from Canadian Actors.* Oxford University Press. Used with permission.

Denis O'Hare: As told to Louis Zorich by Denis O'Hare.

Chapter Six: There's No Business . . .

Jimmy Dean: As told to Louis Zorich by John Styx.

Jerry Orbach: Shewey, Don and Susan Shacter. 1986. *Caught in the Act: New York Actors Face to Face.* New American Library. Used with permission.

Olympia Dukakis: As told to Louis Zorich by Olympia Dukakis.

Jessica Lange: Jeffries, J. T. 1986. *Jessica Lange: A Biography.* St. Martin's Press.

Max Weinberg: *Friars Epistle,* September 17, 2004.

Al Pacino: *People Magazine,* December 13, 1999.

Cole Porter: Milton, Frank. 1985. *Name Dropping*. E. P. Dutton.

Roma Downey: *National Enquirer.*

Charlie Chaplin: Niven, David. 1975. *Bring On the Empty Horses.* Copyright © 1975 by David Niven. Used by permission of G. P. Putnam's Sons, a division of Penguin Group (USA) Inc.

James Woods: Shewey, Don and Susan Shacter. 1986. *Caught in the Act: New York Actors Face to Face.* New American Library. Used with permission.

Toni Collette: *New York Times,* March 19, 2003.

Mark Ruffalo: *New York Times Magazine,* November 9, 2003.

Phil Silvers: *Vanity Fair,* April 2003.

Joan Collins: Collins, Joan. 1985. *Past Imperfect.* Berkley.

Jack Lemmon: Grodin, Charles. 1989. *It Would Be So Nice If You Weren't Here.* Vintage Books.

Dane Clark: As told to Louis Zorich by Dane Clark.

Phil Bruns: As told to Louis Zorich by Phil Bruns.

Neva Small: As told to Louis Zorich by Neva Small.

Grace Zabrieski: As told to Louis Zorich by Grace Zabrieski.

Anna Kashfi Brando: Brando, A. K. and E. P. Stein. 1980. *Brando for Breakfast.* Berkley Books.

Sean Connery: Freedland, Michael. 1994. *Sean Connery: A Biography.* Orion.

Cybill Shepherd: Shepherd, C. and A. L. Ball. 2000. *Cybill Disobedience.* Avon.

Mae West: As told to Louis Zorich.

Howard Rodman: Hay, Peter. 1991. *Movie Anecdotes.* Oxford University Press. Used with permission.

Ken Howard: As told to Louis Zorich by Ken Howard.

Rod Steiger: Kinosian, Janet. *AARP Magazine.*

Skip Hinnant: As told to Louis Zorich by Skip Hinnant.

Jose Ferrer: As told to Louis Zorich by Bill Browder.

Harry Hamlin: As told to Louis Zorich by Harry Hamlin.

Sally Kirkland: As told to Louis Zorich by Donald Saddler.

Vivian Vance: As told to Louis Zorich by Olympia Dukakis.

Paul Reiser: As told to Louis Zorich by Paul Reiser.

Joe Elic: As told to Louis Zorich by Joe Elic.

Michael Cacoyannis: As told to Louis Zorich by Michael Cacoyannis.

Hy Anzel: As told to Louis Zorich by Hy Anzel.

Austin Pendleton: As told to Louis Zorich by Austin Pendleton.

Frank Langella: As told to Louis Zorich by Frank Langella.

Anonymous: As told to Louis Zorich.

Goldie Hawn: *Inside the Actor's Studio with James Lipton*, Bravo Television.

William Fichtner: *Madison Magazine.*

Mike Fischetti: As told to Louis Zorich by Mike Fischetti.

George Abbott: As told to Louis Zorich by Donald Saddler.

Kay Thompson: Donen, Stanley. 1996. *Dancing on the Ceiling.* Knopf. Used with permission.

Frankie Faison: As told to Louis Zorich by Frankie Faison.

Sue Mengers: Matson, Katinka. 1976. *The Working Actor.* Viking.

Leo McCarey, Peter Lorre, Charlton Heston, Lucille Ball, Burt Reynolds, Roland Young, and Luchino Visconti: Hay, Peter. 1991. *Movie Anecdotes.* Oxford University Press. Used with permission.

Margaret Cho: Cho, Margaret. 2001. *I'm the One That I Want.* Ballatine Books. Used with permission.

John Curtis Brown: As told to Louis Zorich by John Curtis Brown.

Allen Swift: As told to Louis Zorich by Allen Swift.

Franklin Cover: As told to Louis Zorich by Franklin Cover.

Chapter Seven: Making an Impression

John Guare: *New York Times,* April 11, 1999.

Bruce Willis: Shepherd, C. and A. L. Ball. 2000. *Cybill Disobedience.* Avon.

John Malkovich: Shewey, Don and Susan Shacter. 1986. *Caught in the Act: New York Actors Face to Face.* New American Library. Used with permission.

Orson Welles: Cotten, Joseph. 1987. *Vanity Will Get You Somewhere: An Autobiography.* Mercury House. Used with permission.

Linda Blair: Biskin, Peter. 1998. *Easy Riders, Raging Bulls.* Simon & Schuster.

French Stewart: *Daily Variety,* December 9, 1999.

Henry Fonda: Teichmann, Howard. 1981. *Fonda: My Life.* New American Library.

John Cassavetes: As told to Louis Zorich by Harry Mastrogeorge.

Robert Blake: Tartikoff, B. and C. Leerhsen. 1992. *The Last Great Ride.* Turtle Bay Books. Used with permission.

Fifi D'Orsay: Sondheim, S. and M. Secrest. 1998. *Stephen Sondheim: A Life.* Knopf. Used with permission.

Sergio Leone: As told to Louis Zorich by Margaret Whitton.

John Belushi: Hill, D. and J. Weingrad. 1986. *Saturday Night: A Backstage History of* Saturday Night Live. Vintage Books.

Abe Vigoda: As told to Louis Zorich by Abe Vigoda.

Andy Griffith: *USA Today,* April 7, 1998.

Walter Brennan: Kobal, John. 1986. *People Will Talk.* Knopf. Used with permission.

Morris Robinson: *The New York Observer,* August 22, 2003.

Frances Sternhagen: As told to Louis Zorich by Frances Sternhagen.

Trevor Howard: Knight, Vivienne. 1986. *A Gentleman and a Player.* Muller, Blond & White LTD.

Barnard Hughes: Shewey, Don and Susan Shacter. 1986. *Caught in the Act: New York Actors Face to Face.* New American Library. Used with permission.

Iggie Wolfington: *Equity News,* September 2000.

Dan Aykroyd: Hill, D. and J. Weingrad. 1986. *Saturday Night: A Backstage History of* Saturday Night Live. Vintage Books.

Imogene Coca: *New York Post,* June 31, 2001.

Carol Burnett: Hay, Peter. 1992. *Canned Laughter: The Best Stories from Radio and Television.* Oxford University Press. Used with permission.

Robin Williams: *National Enquirer,* September 14, 1999.

Bob Fosse: Milton, Frank. 1985. *Name Dropping.* E. P. Dutton.

David O. Selznick, Katharine Hepburn, Lucille Ball, Vivien Leigh: Hay, Peter. 1991. *Movie Anecdotes.* Oxford University Press. Used with permission.

Kieran Culkin: *Time Magazine*, September 23, 2002.

Nehemiah Persoff: As told to Louis Zorich by Nehemiah Persoff.

Yul Brynner: Hyland, William G. 1998. *Richard Rodgers*. Yale University Press.

Jayne Mansfield: Anonymous.

Wendy Hiller: Knight, Vivienne. 1986. *A Gentleman and a Player*. Muller, Blond & White Ltd.

Jed Harris: As told to Louis Zorich by Lily Veidt.

Chevy Chase: Miller, J. A. and T. Shales. 2002. *Live From New York: An Uncensored History of* Saturday Night Live. Little, Brown & Co. Used with permission.

Tim Conway: As told to Louis Zorich by Tim Conway.

Mason Adams: As told to Louis Zorich by Mason Adams.

Frances McDormand: *New York Times*, March 2, 2003.

Ed Blake: As told to Louis Zorich by Ed Blake.

Davey Burns: As told to Louis Zorich by Davey Burns.

John Raitt: *Broadway Treasures*.

B. S. Pully: Everitt, David. 2001. *King of the Half Hour: Nat Hiken and the Golden Age of TV Comedy*. Syracuse University Press.

Anonymous: Matson, Katinka. 1976. *The Working Actor*.

Chapter Eight: If Only . . .

Julia Roberts: Spada, James. 2004. *Julia: Her Life*. St. Martin's Press.

James Gandolfini: *Inside the Actor's Studio with James Lipton*, Bravo Television.

Elia Kazan: As told to Louis Zorich by Elia Kazan.

Laurence Fishburne: *New Yorker*, John Lahr, April 5, 2004.

Jack Gilford: Brown, Jared. 1989. *Zero Mostel: A Biography*. Atheneum.

Billy Crystal: Thomas, Marlo. 2002. *The Right Words at the Right Time*. Atria.

Dame Edith Evans: Callow, Simon. 1984. *Being an Actor*. Penguin Books London.

Saul Rubinek: Green, Lynda Mason and Tedde Moore, comp. and ed. 1997. *Standing Naked in the Wings: Anecdotes from Canadian Actors.* Oxford University Press. Used with permission.

Arthur Penn: As told to Louis Zorich by Arthur Penn.

Chris Cooper: *Hollywood Reporter,* 2003.

Erich von Stroheim: Curtis, Thomas Quinn. 1973. *Von Stroheim.* Vintage Books.

Michael J. Fox: Tartikoff, B. and C. Leerhsen. 1992. *The Last Great Ride.* Turtle Bay Books. Used with permission.

Nehemiah Persoff: As told to Louis Zorich by Nehemiah Persoff.

F. Murray Abraham: As told to Louis Zorich by F. Murray Abraham.

Gemma Jones: As told to Louis Zorich by Martin Sherman.

Ed Asner: NPR, Interview, Audition Series, August 2001.

Humphrey Bogart: Niven, David. 1975. *Bring on the Empty Horses.* Copyright © 1975 by David Niven. Used by permission of G. P. Putnam's Sons, a division of Penguin Group (USA) Inc..

Charles Kimbrough: As told to Louis Zorich by Charles Kimbrough.

Bea Lillie: Lillie, B., J. Philip, and J. Brough. 1974. *Every Other Inch a Lady.* Dell Publishing.

Charles Grodin: Grodin, Charles. 2002. *I Like It Better When You're Funny: Working in Television and Other Precarious Adventures.* Random House. Used with permission.

Helen Hunt: *Movieline Magazine.*

Sean Rice / Mike Nichols: As told to Louis Zorich by Sean Rice.

Tony Randall: As told to Louis Zorich by Vernon Schwartz.

Henry Fonda: Teichmann, Howard. 1981. *Fonda: My Life.* New American Library.

Sam Coppola: As told to Louis Zorich by Sam Coppola.

Jack MacGowran: As told to Louis Zorich by Bill Brydon.

Peter Sellers: Lewis, Roger. 1997. *The Life and Death of Peter Sellers.* Applause Books.

Max Weinberg: *Friars Epistle,* December 2000.

Mickey Rourke: *Globe,* May 8, 2001.

Elizabeth Ashley: Ashley, E. and R. Firestone. 1979. *Actress: Postcards from the Road.* Fawcett Crest Books.

Liam Neeson: Baxter, John. 1996. *Steven Spielberg: A Biography.* Harper Collins.

Joan Rivers: McCrohan, Donna. 1987. *The Second City: A Backstage History of Comedy's Hottest Troupe.* Perigee Books.

Joe Pesci: Kelly, Mary Pat. 2004. *Martin Scorsese: A Journey.* Thunder Mouth Press.

Geoffrey Rush: *New York Times.*

Robert Evans: Evans, Robert. 2002. *The Kid Stays In the Picture.* New Millennium Press.

Monica Parker: Green, Lynda Mason and Tedde Moore, comp. and ed. 1997. *Standing Naked in the Wings: Anecdotes from Canadian Actors.* Oxford University Press. Used with permission.

Richard Russell Ramos: As told to Louis Zorich by Richard Russell Ramos.

Roscoe Lee Browne: As told to Louis Zorich by Roscoe Lee Browne.

George Lucas: As told to Louis Zorich by Walter Beakel.

Bob Hoskins: As told to Louis Zorich by Dustin Hoffman.

Willem Dafoe: As told to Louis Zorich by Jason Bosseau.

Bill Hinnant: As told to Louis Zorich by Bill Hinnant.

Burl Ives: *USA Today*, March 17, 1995.

John Corbett: As told to Louis Zorich by Nia Vardalos.

Albert Brooks: *Vanity Fair*, Oct. 1996.

Kathleen Widdoes: As told to Louis Zorich by Kathleen Widdoes.

Anonymous: As told to Louis Zorich.

Juanita Hall: Logan, Josh. 1976. *My Up-and-Down, In-and-Out Life.* Dell Publishing.

Deborah Kerr: Hay, Peter. 1990. *Movie Anecdotes.* Oxford University Press. Used with permission.

Don Adams: Hay, Peter. 1992. *Canned Laughter: The Best Stories from Radio and Television.* Oxford University Press. Used with permission.

Will Patton: Shewey, Don and Susan Shacter. 1986. *Caught in the Act: New York Actors Face to Face.* Used with permission.

Jennifer Darling: As told to Louis Zorich.

Chapter Nine: What!? And Leave Show Business?

John Travolta: *Time Magazine,* July 30, 2007.

Barbra Streisand: As told to Louis Zorich by Jerry Adler.

Peter Finch / Sidney Lumet: *Variety,* April 1, 2007.

Liev Schreiber: *Time Magazine,* August 1, 2007.

David Ackroyd: As told to Louis Zorich by David Ackroyd.

Bruce Willis: *Vanity Fair,* June 2007.

Tom Brennan: As told to Louis Zorich by Tom Brennan.

John Phillip Law: As told to Louis Zorich by John Phillip Law.

Bruce Turk: As told to Louis Zorich by Bruce Turk.

Elliott Gould: *Village Voice,* April 17, 2007.

Anonymous: As told to Louis Zorich by Eric Weinberger.

David Chandler: As told to Louis Zorich by David Chandler.

Tom Kelly: As told to Louis Zorich by Tom Kelly.

Richard Jenkins: As told to Louis Zorich by Richard Jenkins.

Elaine Stritch / Alan Willig: As told to Louis Zorich by Allan Willig.

Fred Coffin: As told to Louis Zorich by Fred Coffin.

Yusef Bulos: As told to Louis Zorich by Yusef Bulos.

Avril Lavigne: *Us Magazine,* July 9, 2007.

Frederick Rolf: As told to Louis Zorich by Frederick Rolf.

Richmond Shepard: As told to Louis Zorich by Richmond Shepard.

Anonymous: As told to Louis Zorich.

Clifton James: As told to Louis Zorich by Clifton James.

Second City / Bernie Sahlins: McCrohan, Donna. 1987. *Second City.* Perigee.

Priscilla Lopez: As told to Louis Zorich by Priscilla Lopez.

Bob Ross: As told to Louis Zorich by Bob Ross.

Jerome Robbins / Carol Lawrence: *Sondheim Review,* Summer 2000.

Christina Zorich: As told to Louis Zorich by Christina Zorich.

Alan Bergman: As told to Louis Zorich by Alan Bergman.

Richard Herd: As told to Louis Zorich by Richard Herd.

Jonathan Freeman: As told to Louis Zorich by Jonathan Freeman.

Len Lesser: As told to Louis Zorich by Len Lesser.

Kate Buddeke: As told to Louis Zorich by Kate Buddeke.

Dennis Creaghan: As told to Louis Zorich by Dennis Creaghan.

Mario Lanza: Cesari, Armondo. 2004. *Mario Lanza: An American Tragedy.* Baskerville Publishers. Used with permission.

David Gardner: As told to Louis Zorich by David Gardner.

Linda Goranson: Green, Lynda Mason and Tedde Moore, comp. and ed. 1998. *Standing Naked in the Wings: Anecdotes from Canadian Actors.* Oxford University Press. Used with permission.

George Guidall: As told to Louis Zorich by George Guidall.

Louis Zorich: As told by Louis Zorich.

Jay Thomas: As told to Louis Zorich by Jay Thomas.

Shelley Winters: As told to Louis Zorich by Bob Heller.

Kirk Douglas: As told to Louis Zorich by Walter Beakel.

Clint Eastwood: As told to Louis Zorich by Mr. Eastwood.

William Andrew Jones: As told to Louis Zorich by William Andrew Jones.

David Niven: Niven, David. 1975. *Bring On the Empty Horses.* Copyright © 1975 by David Niven. Used by permission of G. P. Putnam's Sons, a division of Penguin Group (USA) Inc.